ALL WE NEED
IS A PAIR OF PLIERS

Advanced Praises for this remarkable story of a lost young man transformed into a servant of the Lord...

"All We Need is a Pair of Pliers is an incredible true story of a young run-away boy searching for adventure and excitement from coast to coast. His day-to-day survival—dependent upon any type of instantaneous, sometimes dangerous or illegal activity—makes this a picturesque and adventurous read for all ages. Throughout Mark Richard's young life, God's hand was orchestrating people and activities that would lead to him to discover his God-given destiny in his current adventure: traveling the world and providing mobility to the poorest of the poor with profound disabilities. It is with pleasure that I highly endorse Mark's first book, *All We Need is a Pair of Pliers*, as an excellent and inspiring read for all ages. My best wishes and prayers for direction and protection for Mark in his future endeavors."

—**Mary Tieken**, Ph.D., Co-Chair and
Trustee of Children's Medical Ministries

"I loved the book! What a well-written and compelling story of triumph and redemption. A must read for anyone. I couldn't put it down."

—**Bruce Carroll**, Grammy and
Dove-Award winning singer and songwriter

"Mark is a friend and brother in Christ whom I have known personally for many years. His story is replete with miracle after miracle of God's guidance, provision, and grace. It should serve as an encouragement to step out of our comfort zone and experience the amazing things the LORD will do with someone who will simply lift their hand and say, 'Here am I Lord, send me.'"

—**Kirk Martin**, pastor of Alliance Christian Center

"Shortly before meeting Mark Richard, Hope Haven, Inc. was presented with the opportunity to support people with disabilities beyond its familiar territory of Iowa to include the Dominican Republic and Romania. Upon partnering with Mark, we came to realize that our vision was too narrow. At times engaging, at times challenging, this man of God pushed us to reach out to people throughout the world. His passion to offer opportunity through mobility advanced the lives of people worldwide, and stretched those of us at home to serve the Lord beyond anything we could imagine. His story just may stretch your vision too!"

—**David R. VanNingen**, Retired CEO Hope Haven, Inc.

"I have known Mark for about twenty-five years, from when he had come back from Guatemala as a missionary. He had a burden to take wheelchairs back to the disabled. I met him at a prayer meeting. From those early days of collecting, repairing, and taking wheelchairs to Central America, now more than a 100,000 have been collected and sent around the world. But then came the building of wheelchairs using the disabled and even prisoners. God has blessed. But now God has the BeeLine wheelchairs. What a wonderful vision God has given through Mark. What a wonderful way to take the gospel to hardly reached people groups. What a wonderful way to help them and empower them to do God's work. Can you imagine taking this help to the disabled around the world? Oh yes!"

—**Dr. Michael Francis,** Cleveland Clinic (retired)

ALL WE NEED
NEED
IS A
PAIR OF
PLIERS

A DIVINE
APPOINTMENT

MARK RICHARD
& JUNE GASTON

NASHVILLE

NEW YORK • LONDON • MELBOURNE • VANCOUVER

ALL WE NEED IS A PAIR OF PLIERS
A DIVINE APPOINTMENT

Published in New York, New York, by Morgan James Publishing. Morgan James is a trademark of Morgan James, LLC. www.MorganJamesPublishing.com

ISBN 978-1-63195-224-1 paperback
ISBN 978-1-63195-225-8 eBook
Library of Congress Control Number:

Cover Design by:
Rachel Lopez
www.r2cdesign.com

Morgan James is a proud partner of Habitat for Humanity Peninsula
and Greater Williamsburg. Partners in building since 2006.

Get involved today! Visit
www.MorganJamesBuilds.com

To my good friend, Carl DuRocher,
without whose influence I would not have
pursued the needs of wheelchair users
throughout the world.

CONTENTS

ACKNOWLEDGMENTS

We would like to thank our publisher, Morgan James Publishing, and especially Dave Sauer and David Hancock who, because of their patience and encouragement, insured that this story would be published. We would also like to thank Cortney Donelson of vocem for her patience, encouragement, and the fantastic editing work that she did for us.

A huge thank you to those whose lives positively impacted Mark's story, especially those whose unfailing belief in him helped him to develop the ministries that he's led.

We would also like to thank the organizations that saw and encouraged Mark's vision, including Joni and Friends, Wheels for the World, and Hope Haven, International.

And last, too numerous to mention, are the many men and women who gave generously and risked much to help Mark on this divinely appointed journey.

INTRODUCTION

It seemed like a good idea at the time, but I had three days in the hospital to regret it. When I was fourteen, my younger brother David was getting into a lot of trouble. Mom's working hours were long, and we had very little supervision. He had most recently broken into a gun club and stolen beer and gunpowder. The beer was an immediate reward, but the gunpowder provided opportunities for endless enjoyment. We went to a nearby construction site and "borrowed" a truck that we used to pick up the stolen goods that were hidden in some woods near the gun club. I had very little experience driving, with most of it behind the wheel of a tractor. This two and a half-ton truck with a stick shift was a challenge for me to drive, but my experience with the tractor helped a little. I hope that the truck still had a bit of its clutch left when we returned it.

We needed to find a place to hide the gunpowder and knew of a dry, shallow well near the rural house we were renting in Prairie du Sac, Wisconsin. We carefully lowered it down into the well and breathed a sigh of relief when it was safely hidden. Our friends had provided dynamite fuses, and we entertained ourselves by making bombs using empty C02 cartridges. We would put wax around the fuses so they were waterproof, throw them off of the bridge going over the Wisconsin River, and watch the dead carp roll up to the surface. Our creativity led to the idea of developing a rocket out of a pole lamp. In retrospect, I'm pretty sure the pole lamp probably had enough gunpowder in it for about five hand grenades. To give us credit, we weren't attempting to blow anyone up but just trying to make a rocket. I lit the lamp section, and my brother Kenny threw it. I thought he was going to throw it as high and far as he could. The top section had a spring in it, so instead of throwing it, he tried to bounce the spring-loaded section off the ground. The open end hit the ground, and by cutting off the oxygen, it exploded and threw me about seventy feet. I landed within twenty feet of our back door. Mom came running out, took in the scene, and with a scream of "Oh my God!" that I'll never forget, she headed back into the house to call the police. I gazed down at the twenty or so pieces of shrapnel sticking out of my body from my feet to my chest, with larger cuts near my knees. Not wanting the police involved, I came up with a better suggestion and informed mom that "all we need is a pair of pliers." There was, of course, a story behind this.

Three years before, when we lived in Canoga Park, California, we were getting ready to load up our 1961 Volkswagen van to drive to Wisconsin. My mom was darning some socks in the living room, and she had a large darning needle sticking out of the carpet. David ran into the living room, dropped to his knees, and the needle went under his kneecap. Panic erupted, but my father came in and calmly said, "All we need is a pair of pliers." He quickly retrieved the pliers from the garage and pulled out the needle. At some point during this current catastrophe, I had the presence of mind to come up with what I thought was a reasonable, proven solution.

Mom still called the police, and I ended up with over eighty stitches and had to be hospitalized, but thankfully, I didn't end up in jail. The police drove up with their brand new Pontiac station wagon. The policeman was more worried about me bloodying up his new car than my condition. At the local hospital, I had to wait for the on-call doctor to show up. Dr. Bachhuber was eighty-four years old, most likely practicing medicine since long before World War I. He had very poor eyesight, and while ashes dropped off of the cigarette in his mouth, Nurse Zuch pointed to where the metal was lodged so he could pull it out. For the next few years, my dad pulled out metal that was left in me, which occasionally rose to the surface. Throughout the ordeal Kenny was crying and apologizing, as he had only two small injuries. I told him to shut up and not worry about it.

Those three days in the hospital, followed by a week in bed, taught me much about being dependent on others. For the next several weeks, I couldn't bend my knee, so being without a wheelchair, I couldn't go anywhere without help—not even the bathroom. My brothers had to help me anytime I wanted to move anywhere. This lesson would prove invaluable as I journeyed through life. As Paul wrote to the Philippians, "Look not every man on his own things, but every man also on the things of others." (Philippians 2:4)

We were created to care for one another.

CHAPTER 1

PREPARING THE SOIL

I come from a long line of hard-working ancestors who, although at times were prominent and prosperous, in more recent generations, struggled with poverty. My mother's family became Dust Bowl refugees from Oklahoma when she was a child. The combination of economic depression and bad weather resulted in many farmers being put out of business. Thousands of Dust Bowl refugees packed up their families and migrated west, hoping to find work. My grandma's family had been sharecroppers from northeastern Texas. It was hard to get her to talk about this time of her life, especially the extreme hunger she and her family had endured. One of the stories she told us, as an example of the dire poverty they had faced, was about killing and eating blackbirds as a young child. The family struggled to survive as sharecroppers and eventually moved to Oklahoma where my mother, Betty, and her sister Freda were born. The family later followed the massive exodus of many others who left the Plains. In the mid-to-late 1930s they moved to California and became migrant workers in the San Joaquin Valley.

A migrant's life was not easy and far from stable. Many Dust Bowl refugees had been farmers, so California appealed to them because of its wonderful climate for growing crops. However, in order to survive, most Dust Bowl refugees became farm hands that followed the harvest up the coast. They picked everything from onions to fruit, following the harvest all the way to Oregon. Eventually, Grandma's family settled in Los Angeles, and she started to work in the sewing factories. After WWII, they made their home in Gardena, California, where my mother was raised in a culturally diverse environment with many of her friends being Asian and Hispanic.

My father's ancestors were North Dakota dairy and wheat farmers. Great Grandpa was a progressive farmer and had the first tractor in the area. Those resilient, tough, French Canadian and German descendants had a strength that was rooted in common sense and a strong work ethic. My grandpa could speak some French and the Native Americans, who were Ojibwa natives, could also speak French. This resulted in strong relationships and horse-trading interactions. Unfortunately, he also shared his whiskey with them. They lived near an Indian reservation called The Turtle Mountains. In the early 1940s, during World War II, my grandfather sold his wheat farm in North Dakota. The family moved to Sauk County, Wisconsin, in order to be closer to one of the uncles and cousins that had moved there previously.

My family's stories demonstrate a history of compassion, diversity, and acceptance in a time when racism was common and accepted. This acceptance of diversity in people permeated my character, enabling me, in later years, to love and accept people from all walks and cultures with no underlying prejudices. This would serve me well as I ministered to the very poor and disabled in developing countries in my adult years. In the Bible, Matthew 25:40b states, "…Verily I say unto you, Inasmuch as ye have done it unto one of the least of these my brethren, ye have done it unto me." God was establishing my character and beliefs, even through my ancestors.

When my mother was seventeen, she dropped out of school to marry my father who was a WWII Navy veteran. Dad was eight years older than her and had served on one of the Merchant Marine Liberty ships as a machine gunner in both the Atlantic and Pacific. They moved to Prairie du Sac, Wisconsin, near my father's parents, soon after getting married. My two older brothers, Denny and Kenny, and I were born in Baraboo, Wisconsin.

In early 1953, I was still in diapers when we moved back to California. By the time she was twenty-five, my mom had given birth to six boys. Chad, David, and Steven were born in Torrance, California. My father bought a house using his G.I. bill in Manhattan Beach. He found work as a maintenance mechanic and joined the Millwrights Union. This began his career of working for companies that had military contracts within the aircraft and ammunition industries. With my parents having six mouths to feed, his paycheck barely paid the bills. It was especially hard when he was laid off for six months. We benefited from caring, generous adults in our community, with an example being when my school principal bought shoes for me. As a child, I remember always worrying about money.

When we were still small, my parents took all of us to the San Diego Zoo and then across the border to Tijuana. The family traveled in the Volkswagen van that dad had bought new at a discount because it had mismatched seats. Our plan was to get haircuts, offered there for twenty-five cents. One of the ways our parents saved money was by having dad cut our hair, so going to Tijuana for a haircut was a treat. My mom had made sandwiches for the family but when we settled down in the van to eat, with the doors opened to the street, some Mexican children showed up and asked for food. My brothers and I sadly watched our mom give some of the sandwiches to those hungry kids. She knew first-hand what hunger was like. We Richard boys knew we were poor, but watching our mom offer these children some of our sandwiches made an impact on us. This was just one example, typical of our mom's generous, loving actions, which helped form our characters.

My father was very practical and prided himself in using common sense and saving money. He had six young boys and a two-bedroom house, and he knew he needed to get us each our own bed. He went to an Army surplus store and bought three sets of Marine Corps bunk beds. The bedroom was still too small so he cut eight inches off of each bed, triple bunked them, and painted them navy blue. Whenever we watched the old TV show *Gomer Pyle*, we could relate to the beds in their barracks.

My upbringing was steeped in the Roman Catholic faith. My dad, who was half French-Acadian and half German, was a devout Roman Catholic. Because of our poverty, we couldn't afford Catholic schools, but dad strove to impose the tenants of his faith on us in every other way. The family strictly followed the rules, paradigms, and traditions of the Roman Catholic Church and the children were held to this strict standard. As a young boy, I spent many hours fearing going to hell, a message of the church that resonated deep within me. The fear of the Lord was preached and practiced and settled into my young soul. Unfortunately, that fear was not balanced with the messages of love, mercy, and grace. I did all I could to keep myself out of hell, including going to confession, praying, and focusing on praying the "Hail Mary," a traditional Catholic prayer that asks for intercession from Jesus' earthly mother. At night in bed, I often thought about eternity—the concept of forever and ever. At one point, I devised a plan that I felt would get me to heaven. I would say three of each of the prayers: the Hail Mary, the Our Father, the Act of Contrition, and then end with the Apostles' Creed. I felt that should be enough to keep me out of hell. Unfortunately, this performance-based belief followed me throughout my childhood and into young adulthood.

I love researching my ancestry and have found many interesting periods of my family's story. My father came from French Acadian roots. In 1654, Michel Richard came to Acadia, now called Nova Scotia, as a French soldier. He married his first wife when he was twenty-six years old and she was only fifteen. She bore him ten children and died after the birth of twins. At fifty years of age, he married his second wife, who was thirty-five years younger than him. His second wife's brother later became his son-in-law after he married one of Michel's daughters. So, his brother-in-law was also his son-in-law.

My maternal grandmother was married four times. Her first husband was Fred Nabors, who was my grandfather. He died when my mother was a baby, and she then married Ed who raised my mother. I have fond memories of Ed as a very small child. Visiting them when they lived in Torrance was always a treat for me. After Grandpa Ed died, grandma married Ted and after being widowed a third time she married Red. So my brothers and I would tell friends that our Grandmother married Fred, Ed, Ted, and Red, and they are all dead.

We lived in the Los Angeles area for about twelve and a half years. Los Angeles was ripe with anger and protests in the early 1960s because of the Civil Rights Movement. One of the more famous incidents that I remember was the Watts Riots. As a result of a black motorist being arrested for drunken driving, a minor roadside argument turned into a full-blown riot. There followed six days of looting and arson, which resulted in thirty-four deaths and millions of dollars of property damage. The riots were blamed on unemployment, but a later investigation strongly indicated police racism.

Events such as these made a strong impact on our family, as we were exposed to blatant examples of racism over and over. My mom's best friend was a black woman named Gwen, whom she worked with at Litton Industries. When my parents decided that they couldn't afford to stay in Canoga Park and wanted to move the family back to Wisconsin, we put our house up for sale. When Gwen and her family came to visit, the neighbors started rumors we were selling our house to a black family. Racism again reared its ugly head. My mom was a city girl and loved California but agreed with my father, and we moved back to the Midwest in January of 1966. Unfortunately, dad started drinking and within a year my parents were divorced.

When my family moved from Canoga Park, California, to Prairie du Sac, Wisconsin, we landed in a community where we were considered hoodlums. When we got there, our dad had to take us to buy winter coats. We didn't have any winter clothing and were on a tight budget. On sale, at a discount store in nearby Baraboo, were black vinyl jackets. Dad bought these imitation leather jackets that, unfortunately, helped make us look the part. Ironically, my dad had very high standards when it came to our manners, how we treated others, and our knowledge of right and wrong, so our actions didn't fit the reputation we acquired based on our appearance.

We rented a house that had a coal and wood furnace in the basement. Our dad believed in hard work and had actually wanted a farm. He bought a bow saw and some slab wood at the local saw mill and built a sawhorse. Dad had sold the VW and bought a truck in California to pull the U-Haul to Wisconsin because the VW couldn't tow. He would take our 1958 Dodge panel truck to the sawmill to pick up slabs of wood. He had us cut the slabs down to length when we got home from school. The sawmill would have done this for him, but he wanted us to learn how to physically work hard.

This community was very insulated, and it seemed like the trouble-making kids gravitated toward us. In addition, coming from California where the schools had lower standards, we were likely in the wrong grades. Looking back, I suspect if we'd been tested, we would have all been moved back a grade. Immediately, we were at a disadvantage, struggling from the first day with the academic demands.

Living in a small town was not all bad, as we could find opportunities for interesting work. For example, we helped a local dairy farmer just two blocks from our house. From cleaning the manure off the dairy parlor floor by shoveling it into the spreader to putting up hay and laying irrigation pipes in the sweet pea fields, we learned what hard, physical work was. I was only thirteen years old, but one day the farmer hitched both tractors to hay trailers, put me on one of the tractors, and told me to push in the clutch. He put it in gear and told me to wait until he took off and then let out the clutch and follow him. He ran to his tractor and took off out the driveway and down the county road for about a mile. That was my first lesson on how to drive a tractor. To a Wisconsin dairy farmer, every thirteen-year-old should already know how to drive a tractor.

I later learned we had lived only two blocks from my future wife, Sandy. Her brother Keith was a year older than me and in Kenny's grade. Sandy's parents and my parents shared exact ages, with both fathers being eight years older than their wives. All four worked in the ammunitions plant, with Sandy's father being a supervisor over my mom and a thousand others. Sandy was only five years old, much too young to garner any attention from young, ornery boys!

When we had first arrived in Prairie du Sac, Wisconsin, we lived just two blocks away from the Harvey's. Sandy remembers overhearing her mom warning her two older sisters to "stay away from the Richard boys." We already had a reputation and Sandy's mom was wary of us.

CHAPTER 2

WEEDS IN THE CROP

The divorce was devastating. Dad rented a cabin a mile away. We were still able to see him, but as much as I loved my mom, it made me bitter toward her. In looking back, this anger and bitterness led to my rebellion. Anger that festers gives the devil a "toehold." The Lord knows this and counsels us, "Let all bitterness, wrath, anger, clamor, and evil speaking be put away from you, with all malice." (Ephesians 4:31, NKJV) I was a young teen boy at a time in my life when I desperately needed the stability of my home. It made me mad at the world. All the things I was told I shouldn't do, such as smoking, cursing, and drinking, were things the adults in my life were doing. This led me to associate these actions as grown-up behavior, and I wanted to grow up. So when adults said drugs were wrong, I assumed they were lying about them too. In this predominantly German community, drinking was a common thing to do. For me, using alcohol was an easy entry into using other substances. Even when I was only fourteen or fifteen, I looked like I was eighteen and could get served beer in bars. Alcohol quickly became an important part of my life.

In the spring of 1967, when I was in the eighth grade, a counselor came to our junior high school. He asked for the names of five students who were considered high risk. Because of my behaviors in reaction to the devastating divorce, feeling like an outsider, and academic struggles in school, I was at the top of their list. They chose four of my friends and me. Unfortunately, just hanging around with kids who were often in trouble had given me a bad reputation. At this age, to some extent, kids are who they hang out with. We attended this class once a week for a whole semester. The strategy of this class was probably the early version of the "scared straight" philosophy. The class led up to a field trip to the Wales School for Boys in a suburb of Milwaukee. This was done in an effort to scare us. I already knew about this school because my brother Denny was living there. He had gone from foster homes to the Job Corps and then to Wales. In a similar effort, they had taken Denny to the Green Bay Reformatory, an adult prison, to scare him. It actually did work for him. I think the juvenile court judges saw us not as bad kids who were hurting others, but rather as rebellious kids who were, simply hurting ourselves. This would come into play again in the future, when David stole a car. He, also, would experience mercy from a judge because he was helping other kids at the time. Unfortunately, we both fell between the cracks and soon ended up in the drug culture.

Summer days in Prairie du Sac offered plenty of opportunities for mischief, which unsupervised fourteen- and fifteen-year-old boys could get into. Prairie du Sac was along the Wisconsin River and had railroad tracks that we knew went to Badger Ordinances, but we also thought the trains went to Baraboo. Every day, there was a train with only five or six cars that would stop about noon and the crews would have lunch at the diner. One day, there was an empty boxcar, along with the usual coal and sulfur cars, which were used to make gunpowder. So three friends and I decided we would jump on the boxcar and get off near Baraboo before it went into the powder plant. After about a half hour, the train stopped, and we looked out and found ourselves facing a guardhouse and gate, going into the powder plant. To avoid being seen, we waited until we entered the plant to jump off. Unfortunately, we were spotted but were able to run through the hay and cornfields and woods until we made it to the perimeter fence to the south. We took off our shirts and laid them on the barbed wire to climb over it without getting cut. We managed to get back to town without been noticed. That evening my mother told us that some terrorists broke into the plant but weren't captured. We kept quiet and were never caught.

A couple of years later, the New Year's Gang, which included the Armstrong brothers, stole a Cessna 150 and dropped three bombs on the plant in protest of the Vietnam War. Fortunately, they did not detonate. The plant worked around the clock so it would have been tragic had one of the buildings blew up with all of the employees in it.

When I was in ninth grade I often skipped school and stayed home. One day the principal came out to the house to find me. When he entered the house, the stereo was blasting the Beatles's "Sargent Pepper." I was out behind the house in the woods and he found me. He called the police and asked them to take me to the local jail in order to scare me. They took me to Baraboo, the Sauk county jail fifteen miles away, hoping to "scare me straight." They believed I'd be there a couple of hours until my probation office came and got me. Unbeknownst to them, my probation officer was on vacation, and I ended up sitting in the jail for several days. They actually felt terrible about it.

Just a year later my probation officer, Patrick Liston, wrote, "You have had sufficient warning about breaking probation restrictions. But I shall warn you again. Any further violations will result in your detention and commitment to Wales School for Boys." At this point, my rebellion was full-fledged. I watched cartoons on the television and read in the newspapers' comics of adults making fun of long-haired guys holding up signs with the words "peace" and "love." Those guys and their message appealed to me. I knew there was something missing in my life and was searching for it. I adopted the hippie lifestyle, and my substance abuse moved from alcohol to marijuana. By the age of fifteen, I had tried psychedelics and intravenous drugs. Crystal meth was the first drug that I shot up.

I came from a family where learning problems were prevalent and I struggled in school. When I was in the ninth grade, I was still reading at a fifth grade level. Ruth Hart was teaching at my high school and took a special interest in me. Ruth and her husband, William Osborne Hart, had been missionaries to Sioux natives in Minnesota when they were first married and had returned home to

Wisconsin to teach. She facilitated a move for me into a special reading class with two other kids who probably had dyslexia or a learning disability. Ruth encouraged me, spent time with me, and let me know that I was valuable to God. She was an incredibly compassionate woman whose care and nurturing continued to build on my fledgling faith.

Ruth Hart's husband, William, was very active in the Farm Labor party. They invited us to the meetings, and we'd occasionally go with them. One of the families, the Dar's, was a farming family. They would invite my brothers and me over, and we would help them on the farm. Because of their socialist ideas, they would feed us like kings around the farm table, but instead of money, they gave us geese in exchange for our work. The socialist way of thinking appealed to us, but we were pretty disappointed when we didn't get paid for our work. My mother was a city girl and had no idea what to do with the geese. This experience also introduced us to some of the socialist radicals from Madison, about thirty miles away. We were soon spending time at the Students for a Democratic Society (SDS) house on University Avenue. This was just before the division of the SDS evolved into the Weather Underground. I think they were very impressed with our rocket-turned-into-bomb escapade.

In June of 1968, my mom moved our family to Madison, Wisconsin. Her goal was to get us back to California, but it was to be a dream that would never come to fruition. It wasn't until nearly fifteen years later that she was able to move back. In Madison she ended up commuting for an hour and twenty minutes to Badger Ordinances, the powder plant where she worked. Unfortunately, the lack of supervision continued and our behavior escalated. She wanted to go back to school in order to get a better job, so she developed a plan to improve our lives. Mom went on welfare, completed her GED, and then went to school to become a technician—one that stored data on computers. Although the family would never be considered wealthy, her new job afforded a less chaotic life and provided more time with her children. Kenny and I both went to the same school for our GED and were even in some of the same classes as our mom.

In retrospect, I believe the learning characteristics I have, which proved detrimental in a school setting, have actually enabled me to have the fruitful life I've led. My hyperactive personality, paired with a strong work ethic, has been essential to what I've accomplished in my life and, in similar ways, what my brothers have accomplished in their lives. I think of the apostle Paul who, as a zealot, had the personality our Lord Jesus knew would fit well with what he would be asked to do—bring the Good News to the Gentiles. Paul demonstrated his extreme passion and commitment to his beliefs when he was persecuting The Way, the first Christians who were following Jesus. Paul's personality didn't change when he came to faith in Jesus, and Jesus was able to use those characteristics to change the world. In a small way, I believe the "disabilities" the Lord has gifted me with have been essential to being successful in the work He's asked me to do. The Lord's view of us differs from the cultural view. "For you created my inmost being; you knit me together in my mother's womb. I praise you because I am fearfully and wonderfully made; your works are wonderful, I know that full well." (Psalm 139: 13–14, NIV) Years later my former pastor, who had known me for years and watched me develop the wheelchair movement, affectionately called me the "Apostle of Wheelchair Ministries." I felt humbled and honored.

When we moved to Madison, our school and social lives didn't improve as this community considered us hippies and socialists. I went to a very conservative, "redneck" high school where prejudice was rife. I was mentored to be a high school anti-war organizer by the local movement, indirectly associated with the SDS. The SDS was a student activist movement in the United States that was one of the main organizations of the anti-government and anti-war movement. We tried to get other kids involved, had weekly meetings, and went to the demonstrations at the University of Wisconsin. In Chicago, at the National Democratic Convention, riots erupted. We joined a peaceful demonstration in Madison, representing the high school students, and organized our own group to march in protest of the war.

My anger fueled my emotions, and seeing no other solution, I ran away from home twice. The first time, in September of 1968, I was arrested and held in the Villa Park, Illinois, city jail for being a runaway. The second time I was arrested, handcuffed, put in a paddy wagon, and taken from Old Town Chicago to the Cook County Detention Center, known as the Audy Home. The Audy Home is now called the Cook County Juvenile Temporary Detention Center.

This was not a good place for a skinny, longhaired, white kid from a small town in Wisconsin. I was in there for two days and experienced intimidation and threats of physical violence, which scared me half to death.

Once back home, I continued to skip classes, especially gym. The gym teacher enjoyed setting the class up so that I was in a position of getting beat up, one way or another, by the other students in the class. The day I turned sixteen, the vice-principal called me in and told me that if I skipped one more class, I was done with school. Knowing I couldn't return to the gym class, I cleared out my locker and left. I went to the parking lot to wait for my friend to get out for lunch, so that I could convince him to go to downtown Madison with me. I rolled a joint of marijuana in yellow Zig Zag paper and began to smoke. I decided to light up a cigarette, also, just in case a teacher saw me smoking. No sooner did I light the cigarette than a teacher came up behind me and said, "Now I've caught you smoking a cigarette." I took the hand I had the joint in and crushed it out. I am still amazed at what a close call that was.

About three weeks later, early in January of 1969, I had done some LSD with my brother Denny and we had the bright idea that we should hitchhike to California. Denny had just returned from California a few weeks earlier, having gone there immediately after he had turned eighteen. He had spent time just hanging out and getting into trouble with our old friend, Keith Green, and wanted to return. We had enough money to buy one-way tickets to Bloomington, Illinois, a town that was 200 miles south of Madison. Bloomington was on Route 66, the highway that would bring us to California, so we took the late-night Greyhound bus to Bloomington and started hitchhiking. The next day we made it to the Ozarks in southern Missouri. The weather was cold and snowy and we were tired and hungry. We couldn't get a ride. After a while, Denny speculated how nice it would be if a hippie bus picked us up, one going to California. It wasn't five minutes later that a painted-up old hippie bus pulled over. As we were getting in, we asked them where they were going, and sure enough, they were headed to Santa Barbara, California. Denny asked if we could get off at the Topanga Canyon Boulevard exit. They agreed and three days later we made it to California. The bus was a late 1940s vintage bus driven by a hippie couple that made their money doing leatherwork and selling crafts. When we got off at

Canoga Park, California, in Los Angeles, we were less than five miles from Keith Green's house.

We had gone to school with Keith at Capistrano Ave Grade School. At eleven years old, he had been the youngest singer-songwriter to have a recording contract with Decca records. Denny had stayed connected with him. Keith eventually became a Christian singer-songwriter who tragically died in a 1982 plane crash. At this time, however, we still believed he was living at home. Keith was also involved in the drug and hippie culture. Denny knew better than to knock on his parents' door. They knew about Denny and disapproved of Keith hanging out with him.

When we got within a few blocks of his house, we went into a Baptist church to try calling him. Two of the pastoral staff greeted us and told us that we could use the phone if we said the "sinner's prayer." The sinner's prayer is a prayer that many pray when they repent and come to Jesus. Denny got mad and refused, but even then, I knew I needed salvation. There was always a feeling of emptiness in me, and deep down, I knew I needed the Lord. I agreed to pray with them and recited the sinner's prayer. My prayer went something like this: "Jesus, I now realize I have sinned against you. Please forgive me of my sin. Please come into my life and change my heart. I want you to be my Savior. In Jesus name I pray, Amen."

In my life, it took another two years after I prayed the sinner's prayer before I totally gave my life to the Lord. I didn't need somebody to tell me that I was a sinner. I knew that because I wasn't at peace. "There is no peace, saith my God, to the wicked." (Isaiah 57:21)

The pastors let us use the phone, but no one answered at Keith's house. Later, we did knock on his door and his mother said he was in Oregon. Initially we thought she was just trying to get rid of us, but eventually we found out that it was the truth. Keith really had run away to Oregon. When he became a popular, powerful Christian singer, he talked about running away at the age of fifteen in search of truth at his concerts.

As a young Christian, Keith started reading Charles Finney, a revivalist and evangelist, and sought out men of God like Leonard Ravenhill, Winkie Pratney, and David Wilkinson. Unlike most of the Jesus Movement singers who had little or no accountability, Keith surrounded himself with others who would hold him accountable. It made him mature beyond his age. You can see his deep understanding of service and obedience to God in his lyrics.

We ended up going to an old neighbor's house, the Mankowitz family, and stayed a couple of nights. Their son Joe, who was a low-rider, gave us a ride to Gardenia where our grandma was, but with the criteria, we had to "low ride" in his car, a 1960 Chevy. This meant that we had to sit as low as possible in the seat, barely able to see over the dashboard. I ended up getting a job with some other old neighbors, the Halls, from Manhattan Beach who had a candy factory. We had sold candy door to door before Halloween when I was just 10 years old and helped box candy after school. The Halls were Mormons and their two older sons were hard-core surfers but not so hard-core that they would still do the missionary service expected by their faith. At this time, they needed extra help to get ready for Valentine's Day and Easter. Fortunately, they had work for me for over a month. My job ended when one of their daughters started showing an interest in me.

On the weekends, I would go and meet Denny who was hanging out on the Sunset Strip, just being a hippie. One weekend in February, Denny convinced me to invest my paycheck in buying some mescaline, a hallucinogenic drug made up of ground-up cactus called peyote. Being an aspiring businessman, he planned to sell it and make money as a drug dealer. It was awful. We quickly found out that we weren't good at selling drugs. Our biggest catastrophe occurred when we went to a coffee house on the Strip and tried to sell it. It turned out that the coffee house was a Christian coffee house and part of Arthur Blessitt's ministry.

Arthur Blessitt was known as the "minister of the Sunset Strip." His goal was to share Jesus with the hippies and other young people on the Strip. Initially, he just walked the streets sharing about Jesus with whoever would listen. He eventually preached in the nightclubs and on stage at rock festivals. He went to the gangs and ministered to all the people groups he encountered. Arthur and his friends started a coffee house called 'His Place' in early 1968. According to Arthur, Jesus called him to make a cross and hang it on the wall of the building. Over the next years, they moved four times, facing battles with the law and club owners. The gospel prevailed and a mighty Jesus awakening took place on the streets and became part of the Jesus Movement. So obviously, this wasn't a good place to sell drugs, but it helped reveal to us that drug dealing might not be our calling.

As I was immersed more and more into the culture of drugs, several incidents occurred that probably changed the direction of my life. While at the candy factory in February of 1969, I got to know one of my coworkers, a heroin addict. At different times throughout his shift, he'd go to the bathroom to shoot up. Watching him really left an impression on me and made me reconsider whether using hard drugs was the right thing to do. In spite of this, Denny convinced me to try heroin. We went to Redondo Beach and were going to buy some heroin to try. I looked older than Denny, even though I was sixteen and Denny was eighteen. Usually drug dealers couldn't care less how old customers were, but this one asked. When we told him our ages, he refused to sell to us. This was a blessing from God. It was such a rare thing that a drug dealer wouldn't sell to someone with money. It had to be yet another divine intervention. I give God the glory for directing us to that dealer. Getting involved in heroin could have totally changed my life. "Concerning the works of men, by the word of Your lips, I have kept away from the paths of the destroyer." (Psalm 17:4, NKJV) The Lord's hand was on me.

After my job ended in late February, we decided to hitchhike to the Haight-Ashbury area in San Francisco. Haight-Ashbury was a district in San Francisco that had been home to the "Summer of Love" in 1967. We arrived at The Haight late in the day, expecting to be able to go and camp in Golden Gate Park. The other street people told us we were crazy because the heroin addicts would mug us if we slept in the park. So we ended up going to North Beach and camped on the beach. The Grand Funk Railroad, a popular rock group, was playing at the concert hall, but we didn't have any money so we weren't able to go. However, being homeless in San Francisco had its perks.

We always had a meal at Diggers, a soup kitchen that provided stew and whole grain bread once a day. We ended up meeting two girls from Kansas City who let us sleep on the floor of their apartment. One day I made my daily trip to Diggers to pick up the free food. As I got within a block of the apartment on South Van Ness, a guy came running across the street telling me how Jesus had saved him and asking me if I knew Jesus. He was so bubbling over with joy and enthusiasm that I couldn't decide if he was insane or the happiest person I'd ever met. He told me that he had been a heroin addict and Jesus had saved him. This was the first time someone had really confronted me with the joy of his salvation. The Bible speaks to this kind of joyful testimony. "Oh come, let us sing to the Lord! Let us shout joyfully to the Rock of our salvation." (Psalm 95:1, NKJV)

It wasn't long until we decided to work our way back to Wisconsin, but first, we decided to go to Portland, Oregon, to visit some cousins. After we left San Francisco, we started hitchhiking. We got picked up by a couple of hippies going up the Pacific Coast Highway. I was still smoking cigarettes, but these guys were "natural" hippies. They scolded us for smoking and it really impacted me. It turned out to be my last cigarette.

After seeing our relatives in Portland, we stayed on the streets and began panhandling, since we were out of money. Eventually we got enough money to go to a grocery store. We walked past a blind man with a tin cup, shaking his cup of pencils. He was totally blind, with sunken eyes. Usually the blind guys had sunglasses on, but this guy didn't. Denny felt so sorry for him that he took all of our change and gave it to this blind man. In my hunger, I hated to see the money go but realized that Denny was following our mom's example many years before.

From Portland, Denny decided to go back to San Francisco but I wanted to go home to Wisconsin. Denny had met a guy who knew the girls we had stayed with in San Francisco, so he went back with him, and they ended up staying through July. On May 30, 1969, they were in Berkeley marching in a war protest with about 30,000 other peaceful protesters.

I hitchhiked to Seattle and spent a couple of days there in the University district. In March of 1969, with thirty-seven cents in my pocket, I hitchhiked home on Highway 12. There were few interstates in those days, and U.S. highways were the only routes back. Somewhere high in the Cascades, I found myself in snowdrifts piling three-fourths of the way up the telephone poles. I was cold, tired, hungry, and alone. I resorted to prayer and eventually found a ride to Idaho. At this point in my life, I believed in God but was not walking with him. I was still in rebellion against my parents, the system, authority, and even spiritual authority. The fact that I was desperate enough to resort to prayer indicated a crack in my rebellion. In Nehemiah 9:17, God's concern and response to rebellion is evident, because they "…refused to obey, neither were mindful of thy wonders that thou didst among them; but hardened their necks, and in their rebellion appointed a captain to return to their bondage: but thou art a God ready to pardon, gracious and merciful, slow to anger, and of great kindness, and forsaketh them not."

The next ride was with a guy who had been drinking. He took me into Montana as far as Billings. He was nice, but he kept drinking as we traveled. After a few hours, he stopped to get another six-pack of beer, bread, and bologna. I made the sandwiches while he drove, and as he continued to drink, he was acting pretty drunk. Looking at me, he decided to explain why he wasn't afraid to pick up hitchhikers. He reached under his seat and pulled out a revolver, and while pointing it at me, he explained that because of his gun, he had nothing to fear. I started praying the "Hail Mary" as fast as I could, and he put the gun away. He meant nothing by it, but when a drunk points a loaded gun in your face, it's a bit scary. He did stop drinking after that and dropped me off in Billings.

A day later in eastern Montana, I got a ride from a farmer in a pickup truck. I hadn't eaten anything since the baloney sandwich. I was too proud to ask for something to eat, but I must have looked hungry because he asked if I needed food. I replied, "I ate a couple of days ago," and this kind gentleman took me to a restaurant and ordered me the biggest plate of pancakes they had. He did as Jesus asked us to in the parable of the Good Samaritan, "You shall love the Lord your God with all your heart, with all your soul, with all your strength, and with all your mind, and your neighbor as yourself." (Luke 10:27, NKJV) By the next evening, I'd made it into North Dakota. It was below freezing and my light sleeping bag wasn't adequate, so I went into a twenty-four-hour laundromat and slept in a bathroom. A couple of days later, I was back in Wisconsin at my mom's house.

CHAPTER 3

WIND AND HAIL

round May of 1969, the word on the street in Madison, Wisconsin was that the police were going to do a big drug bust. My friend and I decided the safest thing to do was to leave town. We headed east toward New York City. I thought, after being at Haight-Ashbury and the Sunset Strip in California, that Greenwich Village in New York City would also be a haven for hippies and street people that were peace-loving and nonviolent. We traveled for three days and hit the city limits. We went to the Village and found out it was a lot different than in California.

We asked some of the other street people where to go to get a free meal. They told us there wasn't any free meal in the middle of the week, but if we waited, the Hare Krishnas provided a meal every weekend in the park. This was a religious sect based on the Hindu god, Krishna. Unfortunately, we knew they were vegetarians, so not wanting to wait that long for a meal, especially a vegetarian one, we headed south. We had only spent one day in New York City.

While still at the Village, we felt a more competitive "dog eat dog" mentality. I witnessed people who were hardened and fighting for themselves, more like a street gang than the hippie groups we were used to encountering. Not feeling comfortable, we started hitchhiking south to Florida. We went to the entrance of the Lincoln tunnel, and it didn't take long to get a ride across to New Jersey. The guy who gave us the ride could see we were hungry and gave us four dollars. Since then, I've met many other kind-hearted people from New York City. I was mad at Jim when he wanted to spend forty cents for a pack of cigarettes. Four dollars could have fed us for a couple of days back then.

We ended up in Jacksonville, Florida, and kept hearing from the hippies about the Peachtree District in Atlanta, Georgia being a good place for street people. After a few days in the Sunshine State, we decided to travel to this stronghold of the hippie movement and took off. Around Macon, Georgia, some farmers gave us a ride. They saw us as potential hires for putting up hay. I wanted to make money and was not afraid of the hard work. I was disappointed when my friend refused. He helped justify the stereotype of hippies being lazy and dirty. That anger helped me put into focus my own understanding of what I was—a hippie—but it didn't define all of me. The work ethic that had been instilled in me was strong and had never gone away. We continued up Highway 41 and ended up getting to Atlanta, needing to make some money. There was an alternative newspaper called *The Great Speckled Bird*, which was extremely popular in the city. Street people could buy copies for twelve cents and re-sell them on the street for twenty-five cents. We sold enough to eat.

The first time we used a public bus in Atlanta, we walked to the back of the bus like we always did in Madison, Wisconsin. We got the strangest looks from the black people on the bus. They had never seen white boys walking to the back to sit. We were not going to walk back to the front but made ourselves at home in the back. A few months later, I remembered this experience when a bunch of buses were parked on East Johnson street a few blocks from the state capital, getting ready to take civil rights demonstrators down south.

This traveling friend had previously been involved in witchcraft. Back in Wisconsin, we had volunteered to be used as guinea pigs by some chemistry students at the University of Wisconsin. These students were making a drug, which people eventually referred to as ecstasy. They'd make a batch, put it in Maalox tablets, and give it to us to "test" the potency. I only did it a couple of times. MDA was like an amphetamine, meaning you'd get really high and couldn't sleep. It was also hallucinogenic, but it made you feel happy as opposed to paranoid or afraid like other drugs, such as STP and LSD, did. One of those trials occurred when I was with this friend. About five of us were walking through the University's Music Hall, which was under construction, and we started to trip. I didn't notice it, but later my friend Tom told me he saw an evil spirit actually possess our friend.

One of my friend's sisters was dating Baby Huey, a black singer from Chicago. A couple of friends would usually hang out at his place with me and smoke marijuana. On one occasion, Baby Huey and his girlfriend shared their marijuana, which was laced with heroin. This was the only time I ever used heroin.

One night in their basement, we were smoking marijuana. We all noticed that one of our friends was acting very strange. All of a sudden we were no longer talking to him but to a demon, Frank, who had died in a car wreck. Later, I realized we were probably talking to a demon that had caused someone to die in a car wreck or commit suicide. Over the next few months, this same friend allowed the demon to totally take over him at times. There did come a time when he resisted. "Submit yourselves therefore to God. Resist the devil, and he will flee from you." (James 4:7) Demons want someone who's yielded, and often someone on psychedelic drugs is willing. When he resisted, it fled, but not before it had done many crazy things and took crazy shapes. One time, I actually spoke to it when he yielded to it. Again, this was another aspect of my life that scared me, and I knew it was not what I was searching for.

My friend, fortunately, had been demon-free during this trip. In Atlanta, we eventually got a job for a small contractor painting a house. I suspected that he was a low-level mafia thug, and I'm not sure if he ever paid us. We lived in an apartment with a teenager who had been living with the Hell's Angels before moving into this apartment. Crash pads were common in those days within the hippie communities. We got to know a few of the Outlaw bikers from a club called the Galloping Gooses, an outlaw motorcycle club that had a very strong presence, mainly in the south.

We spent the weekends at Peachtree Park and after a couple of weeks, we hitchhiked back to Wisconsin. Three weeks from when I left, I returned home. When I walked back into my mom's apartment, she just asked, "Oh, where were you, California?"

I said, "No, I went to New York City, Jacksonville, Florida, Atlanta, Georgia, and Cincinnati, Ohio."

She just said, "Okay."

I was sixteen years old. She loved us but knew we were street smart beyond our years.

In October of 1970, at the age of twenty-six, Baby Huey died from the heroin that had induced a heart attack in a Chicago motel room. Due to a glandular disorder, Baby Huey's weight had soared to over 400 pounds. His band had insisted he go into rehabilitation, but it was too late to save his life. I visited him once when he was being treated at the University of Wisconsin hospital. He was an outpatient staying in a hotel on University Avenue, shortly before his death. This was another tragic casualty of the drug culture. At this time, most of the media attention went to the drug-related deaths of more internationally well-known artists, such as Jim Morrison of the Doors, Janis Joplin, and Jimi Hendrix. All of these singers died within a year of each other. Fortunately, heroin never took control of my life.

One of the defining aspects of the peace movement was the music. In August of 1969 at Bethel, New York, over 450,000 people joined what became, arguably, the defining musical event of the century, Woodstock. The event was planned to be a celebration of peace and music. Some of my friends were involved in playing in bands and writing music and therefore determined to get to Woodstock.

Unfortunately, we didn't have a way to get there, so we decided to hitchhike. Before we took off, however, we went to a local ride board at the Mifflin Street Co-op to see if we could get a ride. We didn't see anything, so we just hollered out, "Hey is anyone going to Woodstock?" Someone responded and told us they were leaving in about a half an hour. We ran back to where we were staying, and I rolled up a pound of marijuana in my sleeping bag. We ended up with eight people in the van, including two friends called Greek and Tom, sharing expenses.

A day later, on the Pennsylvania turnpike, we ran out of gas. As we were sitting on the side of the road, the police pulled up behind us. They opened the back door of the van, which had no seats in it. Unfortunately, we also had some drugs in the van the police would have been interested in. I jumped out to talk to the police, acting nervous and walking around so that they had to turn away from the van, trying to divert their attention. This gave Greek Tom and the others a chance to throw some pills and hashish out of the window. They never looked in my sleeping bag, so I still had my pound of marijuana. Fortunately for us, my presence of mind that led me to distract the police kept us out of jail.

We were some of the first to arrive at Woodstock and the last to leave. We were well situated by the time Richie Havens opened the festival singing "Freedom." The first day I got diarrhea and made a dozen trips to the overflowing outhouses. My friends nicknamed me the "toilet monster." We were never sure if the hotdogs at the food stand made me sick or if it was the uncooked granola, which the Hog Farm was giving away in their free kitchen. Friday and Saturday night we slept under one of the Hog Farm buses. The Hog Farm was a hippie commune from Taos, New Mexico, which was in charge of the free kitchen. One of the Hog farmers, Wavy Gravy, was the master of ceremonies for the concert. We were seated about halfway up the natural dome, listening to the music. On Saturday night, unfortunately, I fell asleep and slept through the entire Who concert. I had been looking forward to hearing them again. Two years before, they were the backup band to Herman's Hermits at Madison Coliseum. Because of the rain and mud, almost everyone left on Sunday, so we were able to get right up to the stage Sunday night, trying to sleep until Jimi Hendrix played on Monday morning.

Woodstock was a real turning point in my life. I thought the music and the drugs would bring inner happiness. They didn't. This experience was similar to when I arrived at Haight-Ashbury seven months before, expecting to find true "peace and love" and only finding a bunch of lost people. I thought this was the best the hippie movement had to offer, and I was still empty.

A few months before, I had made up my mind to stop using LSD and other psychedelic drugs. One of the drugs I had tried was called STD, which the street people said stood for security, tranquility, and peace. When I tried it I only experienced fear and paranoia. Actually, in looking for peace, I found that the things I tried actually brought me the furthest away from peace. Slowly I started seeing that Christians had peace and joy. I started a journey toward distancing myself from drugs and accepting the Lord. As I continued to search, during these years when I was fifteen and sixteen, I hitchhiked through thirty-six states. At this point, my family was fragmented with my mom struggling to maintain any control over her children.

In the summer of 1969, while I had been traveling, my mom moved to the east side of Madison, close to a different school called East High. Since I had good friends there, I thought I'd try doing the tenth grade again. I went to register a few days after I had returned from Woodstock. I had a hunting knife on my belt, a cross earring, long hair, and I hadn't shaved since December. The only reason I had shaved and gotten a haircut even then was that I had been arrested for a curfew violation and was very high on drugs, so I was put in the Dane County jail. Their policy was to shave and give haircuts to all inmates. Being forced to have our long hair cut off was a far worse punishment than spending time in jail.

At East High, I got some strange looks from the office staff, but they registered me anyway. On the first day of school, when I showed up at homeroom, the teacher told me I was not in his class. We argued about it and went to the office to settle it. The first day didn't seem too successful.

A few days later, walking home from school, a kid walked up to me and casually asked if I wanted to fight. Already showing signs of the peace-loving person I would become, I said no and walked away—I had no reason to fight. I managed for a few weeks but eventually decided it was time to drop out and within two months, I had hitchhiked to the West Coast.

I hitchhiked out to California with a friend. After spending some time in Berkeley, San Francisco, and Monterey, we heard about how wonderful Big Sur was with nice beaches, redwood forests, and a good primitive camping area. We camped at Vicente Creek, a part of Big Sur. Big Sur is a series of creeks that come down from the mountains to the ocean.

One day, while collecting firewood, we got into some poison oak. Pretty much all of my body was affected, with one eye completely swollen shut and the other one so inflamed that I could barely see out of it. I convinced some people to take me to the hospital in Monterey. Because of my lack of private insurance, they denied me and told me to go to the county hospital in Salinas. I was actually covered under the welfare program Aid for Dependent Children because my mom was still on welfare, so they admitted me. For five days, I shared a room with a Hispanic guy who had a tube down his throat. Because of the tube, the room didn't smell very good. I basically inhaled the inside of his stomach the entire time! I couldn't eat Mexican food for a while after that. He was a nice guy and it definitely wasn't his fault.

After I got out of the hospital, I hitchhiked back to Wisconsin, alone, in late November. When I was in Evanston, Wyoming, one late afternoon, a highway patrolman pulled over to warn me that a snowstorm was coming, and if I didn't get a ride, I should go into town. Before he left, he asked for some identification. Since I was only sixteen years old and had been on the run, I didn't have a driver's license yet. I had kept my hospital band on and showed it to him. He took me to the Highway Patrol Station because I was underage. They called my mother and the conversation went something like this.

"Did you know that your son, Mark, is out on the highway hitchhiking?"

She immediately replied, "Which way is he heading?"

When they told her toward Wisconsin, she said, "Well, he can find his way home."

They were shocked. They invited me to leave, but I asserted myself, amazed that they would let me walk into the oncoming blizzard. I asked to stay in the jail overnight. They couldn't allow me to stay at the Highway Patrol building but called the city jail and asked if they could bring me over, so I was allowed to sleep in their jail.

However, at 5:30 a.m. during the darkest and coldest part of the day, they woke me up and told me to leave. It had snowed just a little but was windy and very cold. I made it back home in a couple of days. I kept thinking, even as a kid, that I shouldn't have had to ask to stay overnight and was glad that I stood my ground. I learned something about assertiveness on this trip!

In December of 1969, I was arrested during a police raid of a friend's apartment on Lake Street in Madison, Wisconsin. I, along with three of my friends, was charged with burglary, theft, possession and use of dangerous drugs, and possession and use of a hypodermic syringe and needles. I had been involved in a burglary of a dental office a few months before and was using painkillers and barbiturates we had stolen. One of my friends' mothers cleaned the dental office, so he knew how to get in. I was more of a tag along that night. We were taken to the Dane County Jail where they separated the four of us. I knew that I was the youngest, so I told the police I was the only one involved in the burglary to protect the three others involved. The police were glad to get a confession, so they took my word and after three days in jail set a court date and sent me home to my mother's apartment. This was just long enough to get me over withdrawals from the drugs. I had been using lots on Nembutals, a highly addictive barbiturate. Because it was almost Christmas, they had sent all the juveniles home. Even though I had just turned seventeen, I was put in the jail with adults for those three days. One of the inmates told me if I was lucky I would do time at the Fox Lake prison. Interesting enough, I was never sent there, but in a roundabout way, my family is responsible for the wheelchair shop that is in that prison today.

Not wanting to sit still, and with my court date over two weeks away, I then hitchhiked with a friend to South Florida just before Christmas. We were picked up in Miami for sleeping on private property without the owner's consent and were taken to the Dade County Jail for two days. In this jail they had three holding cells. We walked past the first cell that held just black inmates who taunted us. We thought we were going to be put in with them and were very intimidated and scared. This jail segregated blacks, whites, and Hispanics. After a couple of days, we went before the judge, and he gave us a fifteen-day suspended sentence. He ordered us to leave Dade County because if we were arrested again, our sentence would be compounded with these fifteen days added on again. We agreed it was time to get out of Dade County.

CHAPTER 4

SEEDS OF CHANGE

I spent the spring and summer of 1970 going to rock festivals. In April, I went to Sound Storm in Poynette, Wisconsin, the state's first rock festival. I then traveled to Illinois for the Kickapoo Creek Rock Festival in May. The promoters of these festivals used Outlaw bikers to make sure that people didn't sneak in because the sites they chose were in open fields. I was traveling with my girlfriend at this time, and we didn't have enough money to pay the entrance fee, so we hid in the trunk of a '53 Chevy. Once we rolled through the gate, some Chicago Outlaws, a motorcycle gang hired to do security, started banging on the trunk. The driver sped off. Had he not, we would have both been beaten up by the bikers. Six months before, at the Altamont Rock Festival in California, the Hells Angels killed someone in front of the stage when the Rolling Stones were playing. I heard that the Stones were playing the song *Symphony for the Devil* either during or just after the murder.

In June, I went to Iola Rock Festival at Stevens Point, Wisconsin, and the Goose Lake Rock Festival was in Michigan in August. Some of the music helped to develop my non-resistant, conscientious objector stance. The year before, at Woodstock, a band called Country Joe and the Fish sang "The Fish Cheer/I-Feel-Like-I'm-Fixin'-to-Die Rag," in which the lyrics strongly condemned the United States' participation in the Vietnam War.

At Lola Festival, Buffy Sainte-Marie sang "Universal Soldier," which addressed the personal responsibility of every soldier involved in the war. In the lyrics, Buffy spoke to the fact that without the soldiers, there would be no killing.

In later years, when I went to Vietnam with Hope Haven, I wondered how many of the people's disabilities we saw were a result of the gunpowder we shipped from the factory where my parents and in-laws worked. Personal responsibility for decisions cannot be ignored. I had decided to be a peacemaker, and eventually, to tie into Jesus. The song "Eve of Destruction," which was recorded by Barry McGuire five years before, had challenged me even as a pre-teen. The lyrics spoke to the innocence lost for soldiers who weren't even old enough to vote, yet were killing others.

Even as one not yet walking with the Lord, having lyrics like that sticking in my head changed me. The theme songs of the anti-war movement challenged us and made us think deeply. In my search for peace, I was looking in the wrong places.

At this point, I was at the University of Wisconsin in Madison, which was rife with anti-war demonstrations, working on my GED. This program was on campus but not a part of the university. I had been court-ordered to attend classes. This was more of an alternative school. The books we read were by some of the Chicago 7, people who were eventually charged by the federal government with conspiracy, inciting to riot, and other charges related to anti-Vietnam demonstrations. Two of these were Jerry Rubin's book, *Do It: Scenarios of the Revolution* and Abbie Hoffman's book, *Steal this Book*. Another civil rights book, *Black Like Me*, was by John Howard Griffin. It described how a white man disguised himself as a black man and learned what it was like to be black in the South. I could relate to this last book because the year before, I had traveled through Georgia and saw the racism that existed. However, other forces on campus quickly pulled my interest away from my GED. These were the days of anti-war demonstrations. Riots broke out after four students were killed at Kent

State by National Guard troops on May 4th, during a protest about our U.S. troops being in Cambodia.

My good friend and future fellow missionary to Guatemala, Kurt Jackson, was then a Marine doing reconnaissance in Cambodia. Kurt would eventually help us get some of our early wheelchairs and host teams to Guatemala. Kurt and Sally were later challenged to be missionaries by some friends of theirs who were missionaries in the Philippines. After Muslim radicals martyred the wife of those friends, Kurt, Sally and their five children became missionaries in Guatemala in 1987.

The Vietnam War was in full swing and student organizations that opposed the war abounded. On August 24, 1970, the Sterling Hall Bombing occurred, which was committed by four young people as a protest against the university's research connections with the U.S. military during the Vietnam War. It resulted in the death of a university physics researcher and injuries to three others. The bomb was intended to destroy the Army Mathematics Research Center housed on the second, third, and fourth floors of the building. I had just been discharged from University of Wisconsin Hospital, which was across the road from Sterling Hall. I had spent three weeks there because I had contracted Hepatitis B with my intravenous drug use. After giving up the use of psychedelics, I began self-medicating with barbiturates, mainly Nembutal (yellow jackets). Those three weeks in the hospital really impacted me and put me in a place to be mentored by the hospital staff. They took me under their wings and really showed me they cared. I was in a room that had been occupied by another seventeen-year-old, a girl who died from hepatitis just before I was admitted. They told me my case was worse than what killed her. I started to pray during this hospital stay.

At that time, we were squatting in an abandoned frat house on Langdon Street, less than one mile from Sterling Hall. When I heard the explosion at 3:42 in the morning, I told my brother Kenny who was in the same room, "There goes the Selective Service office." Not long before the explosion, there had been a demonstration at the Selective Service Board office by Camp Randall stadium. These were very turbulent times in the United States, and my brothers and I were deep in the midst of the conflict. Years later, when one of the Sterling

Hall bombers, Karl Armstrong, was released from prison my brother, David, was invited to the party.

Between the rock festivals and the anti-war demonstrations, I experienced inner turmoil that resulted in more anger and rebellion. I didn't like the anger, so I eventually stopped going to the demonstrations. Watching students and police fight each other with rocks, tear gas, and billy clubs didn't settle well within me. God was dealing with me and I was seeking the Lord, but I was still looking in the wrong direction.

My nonconformist beliefs were tied into my fledgling Christian beliefs that were very much influenced by the hippie peace movement at this point. I would soon start reading the entire New Testament but was now drawn to the teaching of the Sermon on the Mount. I really wasn't walking with the Lord, but I was developing not only a non-conformist belief but also a non-resistance stance regarding the war. The plant where my parents worked made gunpowder for ammunition, which was being used in the Vietnam War. Dad, throughout my teens and twenties, always wanted me to go to work there because of the good pay and benefits. I resisted and never did. My decision was based on my conscious. I objected to the war and this was one way I could act on my beliefs.

Years later, my beliefs would lead me to a group of discontented Old Order Amish, German Baptists, and Old Order Mennonites. My non-violent stance, paired with the strong work ethic instilled in me by my dad, fit with what the Amish believed. I never shied away from hard work, a character trait that served me well throughout my life. "The sleep of a labouring man is sweet, whether he eat little or much: but the abundance of the rich will not suffer him to sleep." (Ecclesiastes 5:12)

The My Lai Massacre was one of the most tragic acts of violence against Vietnam civilians during the Vietnam War. A company of American soldiers brutally killed the majority of the population of My Lai in March of 1968. Close to five hundred people were executed, which included women, children, and the elderly. High-ranking army officers hid this massacre from the public until March of 1969 when a soldier heard of the incident secondhand and wrote a letter to President Nixon, the Pentagon, the State Department, the Joint Chiefs of Staff, and various congressmen. The letter was largely ignored until later that year, when an investigative journalist interviewed the soldier and broke the story. The My Lai Massacre quickly became an international scandal. Finally in March of 1970, an official U.S. Army inquiry board charged fourteen officers of crimes relating to the incident. Only one officer was convicted. From a sentence of life in prison, he was eventually paroled after serving only a few years. For the people of My Lai, justice was not served. In 2000, while traveling from Saigon to Hue, we passed My Lai on our way to deliver wheelchairs in Hue and Danang. Even though it was more than thirty years later, it—the injustice—haunted me.

Incidents like the My Lai Massacre in Vietnam had the hippie generation questioning not only the war but also the military and the American government. I looked to the Lord, but I wouldn't call my beliefs Christian at that time because I hadn't yet given my life to Him. I was processing and developing during these turbulent times, still searching. Looking back, I believe He was trying to teach me by helping me to develop a solid Christian foundation based on Him and his teachings. He beckoned me to seek Him and increased my desire to be like Jesus.

Someday, I would look back and realize that all of my trials, mistakes, and burdens would culminate in the man I have become and the ministries I was instrumental in developing. "And we know that all things work together for good to them that love God, to them who are the called according to *His* purpose." (Romans 8:28, NKJV)

In 1970, I was staying at my brother Kenny's apartment on West Midthum Street. One of his roommates had a friend, Joyce White. Joyce was an occupational therapist and had worked in Long Beach, California at the Naval Hospital. She was living back in Wisconsin and wanted to go and visit her former patients and friends in California. She asked me to ride out with and her and her friends and then help her hitchhike back home to Wisconsin. On our way out, we stopped in Laramie, Wyoming to see her brothers. Joyce's friends eventually dropped us off in Long Beach.

I went with Joyce when she visited the Naval Hospital. This was the hospital where many of the Vietnam veterans who needed physical rehabilitation were being treated. She gave me a tour and introduced me to some of the guys. Many of these men were missing limbs and this visit left a lasting impact. This was my first introduction to traumatic, physical loss. One of the vets that I met had lost both of his legs. Instead of being depressed or angry, as I would have assumed, he was incredibly upbeat. He told me how he was going to get a three-wheel Harley trike and pick up where he'd left off. After spending time with these men, I realized that my preconceived ideas about physical wholeness were wrong. They taught me that you don't have to have your legs to live a fulfilling life.

Amazingly, five years later in 1975, this friendship with Joyce culminated in a chance to testify. A friend and I were hitchhiking from California to Colorado. At this point, we were part of a traveling missionary group. A man picked us up and we spent the time with him witnessing about our faith as he drove us over one hundred miles. He had broken his jaw, and it was wired shut, so we were able to freely dominate the conversation. He had to stop after an hour to meet with a customer of his. While he was in with his customer, I noticed an envelope with his last name–White—on it sitting on the dash in front of me. When he returned to the car, I said, "You have a sister named Joyce, right?" Joyce's brother was incredulous, thinking we were either prophets or mind readers. Not only was he one of Joyce's brothers, but he was also the one whom I had met five years before. God wants all to come to Him, and provides the path in amazing ways.

CHAPTER 5

DEEPER ROOTS

At the age of seventeen, my life intersected with Jesus in a powerful, new way. I was given a New Testament. I was hitchhiking in California and a young woman picked me up near Seal Beach. The lady asked me if I knew God loved me. I realized that I was very hungry spiritually, longing for God. She told me that her husband, who was at home, knew the Bible much better than she did so she invited me home for a sandwich and an opportunity to hear about Jesus. Once there, the young couple shared the Good News and talked to me about accepting Jesus as my Savior. After giving me a New Testament and a sandwich, they took me back to the Pacific Coast Highway to continue hitchhiking towards Huntington Beach.

The young couple had told me that if I was around the next night they would like me come to a Bible study and gave me a phone number. I continued down to Huntington Beach and was given a ride by a convert to Buddhism who picked me up and took me home with him. While he was doing his meditation, I started reading the book of Matthew. Sitting in a

Buddhist home, the scripture beckoned, and I hungrily devoured as much as I could.

Looking back, I realize the amazing hand the Lord had in my life during this time. First, in meeting the family that gave me the New Testament that provided the Word. Next, while spending time with the Buddhist and contrasting his religion to what I was reading in the Bible, I realized how hungry I was for Jesus. This young man had been a recent convert to Buddhism and meditation. He was a nice guy, but more importantly, the teachings of Jesus just felt right. Watching him meditate, I felt what he was doing seemed empty and was definitely not what I was looking for. I admired his devotion and seeking and hoped that somehow it would be a stepping-stone in his search for Jesus. Last, the invitation to join the young couple in the Bible study provided the beginning of discipleship for me.

I continued hitchhiking that day back toward Long Beach. I procured a ride with a guy in a small car who was traveling up the Pacific Coast Highway. The guy only gave me a ride for a couple of miles because, at a stoplight, I noticed someone with his back to me whose motorcycle boots looked familiar.

I thought, "My brother has boots just like that." Upon a closer look, I realized it was my brother, Chad. I knew there wasn't room for all of us in the car, so I got out. I walked up to Chad and our friend, David Wilson, surprising them. We were all completely amazed that we met on a random corner in Orange County, California, 2000 miles from home. I told Chad that I had been up to visit at the Naval Hospital, where Joyce was visiting. I took them to the Bible study with me that night. This was just one more example of God's divine intervention. Not only has God blessed me with a multitude of miracles and divine appointments, but oftentimes, I have received two or three on top of each other. *Divine appointments come when you're open to the Lord's leading.* When crossroads come, choose Jesus' way. Chad and I were both being dealt with by God. "In all thy ways acknowledge him and he shall direct thy paths." (Proverbs 3:6)

Chad never became a churchgoer, but he has always been Christ-like, demonstrated by his amazing capacity for compassion. He is one of the most Christ-like people I know, particularly in his relationships with others. Chad is a true friend—the guy everyone knows you can count on.

Prior to this, Chad had made friends with a man who was a Christian, one of the earlier Jesus freaks. This friend witnessed to the hippies in Wisconsin, and planted seeds in his heart. Chad had a lifestyle of partying and drinking but was always a good guy. God kept tapping on his heart. Chad collected hundreds of wheelchairs and has been part of over a dozen wheelchairs deliveries, which have benefited many people.

Throughout the '70s, as I attended some Bible studies and read my New Testament, I realized that the religious rituals and traditions which my dad had strictly adhered to were different than knowing my one true Savior. As I hitchhiked around the country, I dove deeper. I spent a long time reading and studying the Sermon on the Mount.

Over the next ten years, whenever I found myself near a library, I would spend hours reading all I could about early church history, the reformation, missionary stories, and stories about believers imprisoned for their faith in communist lands. I immersed myself in reading and memorizing scripture. After I had been reading the New Testament for about six months, I found myself hungry to act on my new faith. I had visited various churches, but most were very traditional and tended to remind me of the masses I had attended as a child. At this same time, there was a new movement in the country, the Jesus Movement.

In Matthew 11:28, Jesus says, "Come unto me, all ye that labour and are heavy laden, and I will give you rest." The hippie movement was actually a generation looking for exactly what Jesus had to offer—rest. Their constant search for peace and rest had resulted in the use of drugs, sex, rejection of authority, and rejection of morals. In their restless searching, they looked the wrong way, which resulted in lifestyles that were damaging and self-medicating. How do you find true peace? Peace and rest can only come from Him, and the Jesus Movement tapped into the growing realization that the path they had taken was not resulting in what they were seeking. God can meet people where they're at, as He wants all to come to Him. Throughout our lives, we will all reach a crossroads where we make the decision whether to follow Him or not.

The Jesus Movement was a legitimate move of God. Unfortunately, when God moves, Satan attempts to move also, which results in a counterfeit choice for people.

Spiritual counterfeits seemed to thrive. Powerful cults included Maharaji and the Divine Light Mission; Sun Myung Moon, the founder of the Unification Church; and the Children of God, later known as the Family. When Maharaji rented the Houston Astrodome in November 1973, we went there to witness. False teachers and prophets led many young people astray, but others truly found the Lord. As time went by, the churches opened up and welcomed these new believers.

I had made up my mind that I was going to serve Jesus, but I was not looking to get plugged into a traditional church setting. My experiences in churches did not lead me to believe they could provide what I was hungry for. In 2007, Zondervan published a book by Dan Kimball called *They Like Jesus but Not the Church*. Others have been bolder, stating they love Jesus but hate religion. This described my feelings at the time. The mainstream churches didn't know what to do with hippies.

Around 1970, I had heard of a house ministry in the Milwaukee area. I considered hitchhiking to Milwaukee to find this group, but I never did. This was the beginning of the Christ is the Answer Crusade. An evangelist by the name of Bill Lowery, with his wife Sara, was ministering to a very small group of Christians. They used a tent and traveled from city to city, preaching the gospel. Our first encounter with them was in the winter of 1973 when we ran into them in Gainesville, Florida. About a year later, they had started doing tent revivals, and we ran into them in Tucson, Arizona. As it turns out, an old friend of mine from Neillsville, Wisconsin, had joined them. He had almost come to Woodstock with me. This was another amazing connection. He had gotten saved and was traveling with them.

They started traveling and eventually broke off into a branch that did crusades in Mexico and Europe. Around 1979, while I was in Madison, Wisconsin, they were doing a crusade, so I had the privilege of hearing Bill preach and visited with him. Some of them had settled down in the north side of Chicago and changed their name to Jesus People USA. I know, like most ministries, they've had their scandals and troubles, but a lot of people were rescued out of the drug culture through them. Unfortunately, living in community was not healthy for their families and the kids who grew up in it. They developed their own rock band, the

Res (Resurrection) Band, and started a Christian rock festival in Illinois. I had the opportunity to visit the Jesus People USA in Chicago three or four times. In the early 1980s, at a crusade in Veracruz, Mexico, I ran into them again.

I was with three friends and we were driving back to the States from Belize in or around 1982, volunteering for some of the Mennonite missions. The Mennonites had VS (volunteer service) workers that typically required a two-year stint. I just came in and helped where I was needed but was not under their mission board. There was a local Baptist mission that had a F250 Ford pickup truck, which was about four years old. Their supporting church in Memphis, Tennessee, offered to do a rebuild on the truck. The head of the mission allowed us to drive the truck to Memphis and leave it at the church. The four of us split the gas. We made it half way through Mexico and started having what seemed like carburetor problems. One of the volunteer service workers was the mechanic for Caribbean Light And Truth Mission and the other served as a mechanic for the Mennonite church in Chimaltenango, Guatemala. Along with these men, Verton and Jason, was Craig, a schoolteacher who was later with me when we found the Mayan ruins. We realized it was a fuel line problem, so they decided maybe the gas tank was dirty. We pulled it out and tried to clean it. After narrowing all the possibilities down, we finally realized that the problem was the fuel pump. We went to the Ford dealership in Vera Cruz, Mexico to get a new one. As it turned out, the Fords made in Mexico have a different fuel pump, which is not compatible with American-made Fords. While there, we ran into the Christ is the Answer Crusade.

When we took off, we would drive for an hour or so and all of a sudden the truck would stop. I suggested that we take the gas tank off and tie it to the roof of the pickup so that gravity would flow the gas right into the carburetor. I had remembered people talking about the Model A or T, describing when they had to back up steep hills because they needed the gravity flow to get gas to the carburetor. In our last-ditch effort, that's what I came up with. Verton Miller always had a little leather pouch with a pair of pliers in it. This was before the leather man tool. (I was the Swiss army knife guy—always had one.) It was amazing how much you could do with a pair of pliers on trucks in the late 1970s. Because I wasn't considered a mechanic, they didn't take me very seriously. But hey, that's the story of my life. "A prophet is not without honor except in his own country." (Mark 6:4, paraphrase)

Finally, after we broke down again on the side of road near Poza Rica, Mexico, Verton and Jason were so desperate that they agreed to try my idea. We quickly discovered there was no way to fasten the gas tank to the roof. So I went to my backpack and pulled out the mountain climbing rope I used on my hammock and tent fly and my camping foam. Before we pulled the gas tank off we took a gallon jug, siphoned water into it, and ran a line to the carburetor. One of us held onto the jug with it siphoning and we drove for a while. It worked and they finally decided to try the gas tank. We put the foam between the tank and the truck to protect the paint. We drove all the way to Memphis with a stop in Springfield, Missouri to drop Verton off. Before I brought the truck to the Baptist church in Memphis, I dropped the other two off at the Greyhound bus station. I then hitchhiked to Lobelville, Tennessee to visit my Amish friends before going back to Wisconsin.

And later, in 1999, we did a wheelchair delivery in San Salvador. We found out the missionary who coordinated it had traveled with the Christ Is the Answer Crusade. They had a huge impact.

I had heard about a different group of Jesus freaks made up of non-traditional groups. I was at a Grateful Dead concert in the Fieldhouse at Camp Randall Stadium at the University of Wisconsin Madison in early 1971. I met an old friend whom I hadn't seen in a while, David Miller. I asked him how his older brother George was doing, and with a look of disgust he said, "He's a Jesus freak now and so is my mother and sister."

He invited me to come and stay but said he understood if I didn't want to be around his family now that they were Jesus freaks. I secretly wanted to go just to hear more about Jesus.

The next week I was an hour away in Janesville, Wisconsin and I went as a guest of David's to his high school class reunion. In the evening, his mother invited me to their Bible study. I let them pray for me but was disappointed that I didn't have a dramatic experience, one where a light came out of heaven or something equally miraculous. This showed me how much I wanted a powerful conversion experience. Soon after, I decided I would just hitchhike south on

Highway 51 and get to I-80 and pray for God to guide me to a Christian group that would take me in. I got to I-80 and tried to hitchhike west. After a half hour of not getting a ride I thought, well maybe God wants me to go east. After another half hour, I started hitching south. I ended up in Carbondale, Illinois, and a guy let me crash with him. I was still reading my New Testament at this time. The next day, I headed back north, thinking I would stop by Janesville again but when I got a ride all the way to Madison I decided to go stay at my dad's in Sauk City. When my dad was at work the next day, I read my New Testament and prayed. Something came over me and I started to cry. I told God I needed Him in my life.

CHAPTER 6

A NEW ROAD

was looking for a group that would mentor me into a different lifestyle. In May 1971, Mike Kovak, an old friend of mine from Wisconsin, and I were walking on Telegraph Avenue in Berkeley, California, and we met a group of Jesus freaks. They started sharing about Jesus with me, and I immediately asked if I could stay with them. They asked to pray with me, and we dropped down on our knees in an alley and started praying. I told Mike I was staying with this group, and he went back to Wisconsin without me and told my family that the Jesus freaks, "took him."

I assumed they were a part of a house ministry where everyone stayed at a central home, similar to a commune. As it turned out, they were a traveling group who were in the area and sleeping in a county park in the Oakland Hills. "And Jesus said unto him, Foxes have holes, and birds of the air have nests; but the Son of man hath not where to lay his head." (Luke 9:58) They were just as homeless as I was! The group had an old Ford pickup with a topper they used to shuttle us to the park. Within a few days, they had a group baptism, and I was baptized at Lake Alice. This group was a community made up of about thirty young people who came out of the hippie, anti-war movement. Very few of them knew anything about the Bible, which actually turned out to be good in some ways because we had a blank slate to start with. I was given a Gideon King James Bible. While reading the Gospels and the book of Acts, we took our commission literally. "So likewise, whosoever he be of you that forsaketh not all that he hath, he cannot be my disciple." (Luke 14:33)

A man named Jim Roberts led this group. Born in Kentucky, Jim Roberts was raised in poverty, the son of a Pentecostal holiness preacher. After graduating from high school, he joined the Marine Corp, making sergeant before he left in 1961. After getting out, Jim' home church rejected him as a preacher because of his extreme views. For the next few years, he moved around the country witnessing to the hippies. In the winters of 1970-1971, he went to visit a preacher named Rufus Sherrill. Rufus believed the Pentecostal church he had been a part of had strayed from the truth, so he moved his family to the Bitterroot Valley of Montana. Roberts thought he should stop evangelizing by simply going from church to church as he had been doing. Instead, he felt called to witness to the hippies and on college campuses. Brother Sherrill told him about the "House of Jesus" in Missoula. Their leaders were two Baptist ministers and a Lutheran seminary student. He was invited to preach a revival. Cecil Barnes, one of the ministers, had a dream that Jim should stay and preach for forty days and forty nights. So, he preached on the University of Montana campus during the day and preached at the House of Jesus in the evenings. When he left, many of the students who attended the university dropped out of college and followed him. They left in a caravan of six cars, one pickup, and an Indian motorcycle, ending up in California.

The group's goal was to move around the country witnessing and making disciples, focusing especially on the street people and youth. We were obeying the command, "Remember thy creator in the days of thy youth." (Ecclesiastes 12:1) In 1971, for the most part, the mainline churches weren't reaching the kids who were coming out of drugs and had been in trouble with the law. Eventually the group split and what was left were about thirty kids and a traveling ministry. For most of us, it was exactly what we needed in our lives. Our leader, Roberts, used his Marine experience with military discipline, which when paired with his Pentecostal background and calling gave us the leadership we craved for the changes we were making in our lives. From the "free love" movement where there were no boundaries, the pendulum swung in the opposite direction and The Assembly actually provided the exact opposite: extremely rigid rules and boundaries. In many ways, we needed this in order to gradually bring our lives back to a more balanced place.

We tried to base our lifestyle on the book of Acts. Only two people out of our thirty had any scriptural training or background. Jim Roberts was ordained in the Pentecostal church and Rick Lockrem was a Lutheran seminary student. The rest of us were ignorant of the scriptures. Jim initially spent time telling us what the Bible meant. Coming out of the hippie and free love movement and having been immersed in the drug culture, we embraced Jesus' words and became totally "sold out" for Him. "Wherefore I say unto thee, her sins, which are many, are forgiven; for she loved much: but to whom little is forgiven, the same loveth little." (Luke 7:45) We were so glad to have the joy and the peace of the Lord. Forsaking all did not sound like a big sacrifice; instead, it sounded like reasonable service.

For the first few years, we stayed in campgrounds, never more than a few weeks in one place. The Army Corp of Engineers would let us stay free for up to two weeks. We'd travel north in the summer and south in the winter. Mainly, we were involved in evangelism, but sometimes we would do some migrant farm work. In the Everglades of Florida and the apple orchards of Washington State, we worked day jobs but considered all jobs as opportunities to do evangelism with the migrants. Within a few years, we focused more on inner cities. We learned how to find abandoned buildings, go to the courthouse to find the owners, and then make deals with them to barter things like cleanup and remodeling in exchange for free rent. This strategy worked in Montreal, Washington D.C., New York City, Boston, Miami, Buffalo, and Seattle. We would maintain them for up to a year or longer, as traveling brothers and sisters would come and go.

Jesus commanded his disciples to go out two by two, which we obeyed. Over and over we learned to trust the Lord for our safety, our basic needs, and our opportunities. In one way, we became pioneers of the modern food bank.

Grocery stores would dump produce and other outdated foodstuff, which we would retrieve from their dumpsters in order to eat and survive. "Then shall the lambs feed after their manner, and the waste places of the fat ones shall strangers eat." (Isaiah 5:17) In 1 Kings, God instructed the ravens, who were considered unclean, to bring food to Elijah. "And it shall be, that thou shalt drink of the brook; and I have commanded the ravens to feed thee there." (I Kings 17:4) We continued to embrace the belief that blessed are the poor and humility was a virtue.

"Take therefore no thought for the morrow: for the morrow shall take thought for the things of itself. Sufficient unto the day is the evil thereof." (Matthew 6:34) In our former lives, self-sufficiency had put us in a position to not have to trust in the Lord. Now, we truly learned dependence on Him for all things. While hitchhiking, which we did often, we prayed each time we stuck our thumb out, "Lord who do you want us to tell about You?" The scariest were the drunk drivers, but I don't recall anyone getting hurt. God protected us. It was a different world and a lot of rides were with Vietnam vets. These veterans were coming back from the war and were pretty confused. They weren't received very well by the United States and didn't have the "hero" welcome veterans of previous wars had enjoyed.

This was radical Christianity. It wasn't firebombing an ROTC or throwing rocks at the police. At the University of Wisconsin, as well as on many other campuses, war protesters expressed their anger by using violence and aggression. Kent State was a good example. When Nixon invaded Cambodia, the campus erupted with violence, resulting in the Ohio National Guard shooting and killing four students. Throughout the nation, police reacted with tear gas and arrests in an effort to contain the protests and violence.

In contrast, radical Christianity involved profound beliefs, such as turning the other cheek and overcoming evil with love. Even today, a lot of Christians are trying to overcome evil with evil, ignoring Jesus' teachings that love is more powerful than hate. In Matthew 5, Jesus teaches, "But I say unto you, love your enemies, bless them that curse you, do good to them that hate you, and pray for them which despitefully use you, and persecute you; That ye may be the children of your Father which is in heaven: for he maketh his sun to rise on the evil and on the good, and sendeth rain on the just and on the unjust. For if ye love them who love you, what reward have ye? Do not even the publicans the same? And if ye salute your brethren only, what do ye more than others? Do not even the publicans so? Be ye therefore perfect, even as your Father which is in heaven is perfect." (v. 44–48)

In Matthew 5:38–39, Jesus tells us, "Ye have heard that it hath been said, an eye for an eye, and a tooth for a tooth: But I say unto you, That ye resist not evil: but whosoever shall smite thee on thy right cheek, turn to him the other also." Earlier, in verse nine, He talked about our role in the world, "Blessed are the peacemakers: for they shall be called the children of God." He leaves little room for argument about how a Christian should respond to evil and conflict. Christians are people who forsake all for the Lord. *If you're following Jesus, you're out ministering and helping people.* In James, he teaches, "Pure religion and undefiled before God and the Father is this, To visit the fatherless and widows in their affliction, and to keep himself unspotted from the world." (James 1:27) Where do people get the idea that strapping a bomb to their bodies is serving God? Our voice wasn't heard then and perhaps, isn't being heard yet today.

The only way to succeed is to fight evil with love. In America, we need to remember who the real Jesus is. It seems we're not being taught anymore about whom He really is. Years ago, in "The Gentle Healer," Michael Card sang about Jesus' tender love for us. He showed it not only through the healing He did while on earth, but for all of us by dying to take our sins away.

Later, other bands reiterated the message. The Ember Days sang "Real Jesus," a song that emphasized how Jesus spoke of peace, died for us, and cared about the poor.

In contrast, protest songs spoke of anger and violence. Rich Mullins further described Jesus' character in his song, "You Did Not Have a Home." He spoke of His love and impartiality to all who came to Him.

I really appreciated songs about Jesus' character.

What is of the devil and what is of God? As Christians, we need to look different than those who do not follow the Lord. Seek and find the real Jesus.

Nowhere in the Gospels does Jesus tell us to expect an easy, prosperous life. Instead, while preparing his apostles, he told them in John 16:33, "These things I have spoken unto you, that in me ye might have peace. In the world ye shall have tribulation: but be of good cheer; I have overcome the world." Jesus repeatedly warned us that the world hated Him and would hate us, too. Jesus wants us to be content with food and clothing—he doesn't even mention needing a house! "Therefore take no thought, saying, What shall we eat? or, What shall we drink? or, Wherewithal shall we be clothed." (Matthew 6:31) He assured us that our Father in heaven knows we need these things, and He will provide.

Instead, Jesus talks about being generous and loving others. In Matthew 25:40, He tells us, "And the King shall answer and say unto them, Verily I say unto you, Inasmuch as ye have done it unto one of the least of these my brethren, ye have done it unto me." Our focus should be on caring for and encouraging those who are struggling, not on our own wealth and comfort.

After being with the ministry for just over two months, I traveled through Wisconsin and stopped at home. My brother Denny, who was newly married, was still struggling with addictions and realized he couldn't overcome them without God's help. He and I drove to Colorado to join up with the traveling ministry. We were in fellowship with a small church in Pueblo, Colorado. We met up with the rest of the group, and I got Denny plugged into the church.

Initially, we rejoiced. He "got saved" and became immersed in spiritual teaching. Unfortunately, in the long run, it turned out to be a bad thing for him. The church became very condemning and embraced legalism, which led to spiritual abuse. Although he did get saved, after a couple of years, he left the church and went back to his old ways. Since he had backslid, he was convinced he could never be renewed to repentance, a false teaching that this church had put on him. Denny spent the following years getting divorced, doing drugs, hanging out with motorcycle gangs, and falling deep into alcoholism.

During this time, he had a very close call. He was a cement finisher in Wisconsin, and at that time, there wasn't much inside work. He was unemployed during the four months of winter. One winter he put his motorcycle on his truck and drove to New Orleans to find work through the union hall. He was in a bar one evening, and one of the Outlaw motorcycle gang members of the Galloping Gooses started mouthing off to him. Denny knew he had to bite his tongue.

Even though he was a good fighter and strong, he couldn't take on the whole gang. So he waited for the guy to go outside and caught him alone and beat him up. They knew who he was, so he flew back to the room he was renting, packed up as fast as he could, and drove back to Wisconsin. Had he stayed in New Orleans, his life would have been in danger. Denny's wild lifestyle of partying, drinking, drugs, and fighting could have easily led to his death. It was God's mercy that spared Denny throughout this time until he could be renewed to his first love—the Lord.

Whenever I was home I would always talk to him about God's mercy, forgiveness, and grace, but he was convinced God wouldn't take him back. He had been taught that he had put the Lord to shame because of his behavior and that he was unacceptable. The church had used scripture to emphasize this point. Matthew 12:45a tells the story of one who was saved but falls back into sin. "Then goeth he, and taketh with himself seven other spirits more wicked than himself, and they enter in and dwell there: and the last state of that man is worse than the first." He was convinced he was going to hell, believing that if you backslid you were going to be seven times worse off than when you first were saved. He was self-fulfilling that prophecy.

It wasn't until January 1992, when Denny came on a wheelchair delivery trip with us, that he realized God could use him, and this began his road to restoration with the Lord. On this trip, we drove our old school bus down to Guatemala with sixty wheelchairs on the storage rack. After the trip, Denny came back to the States and started collecting wheelchairs in Los Angeles and Dallas, Texas. Denny was even responsible for getting our brother, David, involved. David eventually, with my help, founded both Wheels for Humanity and Global Mobility wheelchair charities in California. For the next three-and-a-half years, Denny committed himself to help us collect wheelchairs. It was contagious—his love for people and his passion for finding wheelchairs in California, Wisconsin, and Dallas. In the last year of his life, he was instrumental in starting Wisconsin's Wheelchair Recycling Project (WRP). Based in Madison, it started as an all-volunteer effort to send used wheelchairs and medical equipment overseas. It soon became apparent that there were serious needs in Wisconsin, and WRP now focuses on providing services locally. They have a prison industries program in Fox Lake Prison, refurbishing manual and power wheelchairs with the help of Invacare. It's a low-cost alternative for people with no insurance.

On Thanksgiving in 1994, Denny died. He was only forty-four years old. Some assumed it was a heart attack, but he had never been diagnosed with heart disease. At the time of his death, he was spending time with old family friends, Katie and Phyllis Sticka, in Minneapolis. We had grown up very close to the Stickas. My mom and Phyllis had been single mothers with a bunch of kids. We were almost like a blended family, always doing everything together. Because of the holiday, most of the doctors were gone. They eventually ruled out a heart attack, but a thorough autopsy was never done. Mom always suspected he had sleep apnea. When he'd stay with her in Torrance, there were many times when she'd hear him fighting for a breath in the middle of the night. At his funeral, I spoke. It was an untraditional funeral with a pretty rowdy crowd filled with old hippies and bikers. This was an opportunity for me to testify to his life. Denny's life really was a testimony as to how God could use anyone. As wild and crazy as he was, he was always the gentle giant, defender of the innocent.

Our ministry group was very strict. In looking back, I realize now the magnitude of strictness was excessive, but at that time in my life, it was needed and effective. One of the members of our group turned out to be the brother of the little girl, Sandy Harvey, who had lived down the street from us when we were children in Wisconsin. The first time I remember seeing Sandy at that point in my life was when she was eleven years old and came skipping across a school yard as she was going home to her house in Adams, Wisconsin. She eventually figured out that I was one of the Richard boys who her mother had warned her sisters about. In 1972, Sandy's mom, her brother Keith, her sister Sue, and Sandy went to Tulsa, Oklahoma, where the group had rented a large house near downtown. Soon they joined our traveling ministry.

CHAPTER 7

NEW GROWTH

I n the ministry group I was traveling with we had six people from eastern Ohio. Two brothers and I traveled back to visit one of the brothers who had returned home and was working for Jacob Maendel. Jacob had been a member of the old Hutterites in North Dakota but had left to be part of the Hutterian Society of Brothers. The Plain people and their influence on my life were significant then, and their influence continues to this day.

Jacob was disillusioned with the old Hutterites and wanted something less traditional and more spiritually alive. The Jesus Movement in the United States embraced the characteristics of living in community like the old Hutterites of Canada and the Dakotas. Jacob had moved to the Hutterian Society of Brothers in upstate New York. He soon became disillusioned with the Society of Brothers and moved to eastern Ohio. When he found out about our group and how we embraced living in community, as well as emulating many other like-minded Plain lifestyle ways, he invited us to stay on his farm. This was my first contact with the Anabaptists.

His kids were going to the public high school, and they knew someone who had traveled with us for a short time. That had sparked his interest in our group and he was eager to connect with us. Over thirty of us lived on the Maendel farm in Columbia, Ohio in the spring of 1973 for more than a month. This was our first introduction to the Plain People. One of the Anabaptists' common phrases was and is, "God doesn't have any grandchildren," which spoke to personal belief and personal responsibility for our faith. Jacob and his family have continued to be part of my life over all of these years.

Our ranks grew. We thought if the people we shared the Good News with had truly accepted the Lord as their Savior, they would forsake all and join us. "Then answered Peter and said unto him, Behold, we have forsaken all, and followed thee; what shall we have therefore?" (Matthew 19:27) The message from our leaders was that if a person was saved, he or she must give up their lives for the gospel to follow the Lord. Our definition of a saved person was based on this scripture. Unfortunately, although God was meeting us where we were, we weren't spiritually mature enough to realize that although this was an important transitional step in our lives, it was not all that the Lord had planned for us. In addition, we didn't understand that this was not what He wanted for everyone else.

While traveling in big groups, we also learned how to hop freight trains. There were too many hitchhikers out on the roads, and it became difficult to find rides. We learned the unspoken rules of train-hopping which, when followed, insured that the railroad police would look the other way. If we stayed out of the big cities and didn't ride mail cars or new car transports, we were tolerated. In some cases, the train crews would let us ride in an empty caboose or engine.

As an example of our travels, in 1974, we were camping by a river near Spokane, Washington, at the World's Fair doing evangelism. I decided I wanted to get away for three or four days, like Jesus who often went off alone to fast and pray. I went to the Great Northern train yard, which is the Burlington Northern now, and hopped on a freight train to travel across to Glacier National Park in Montana. For some reason, this train had two cabooses. When we stopped in Libby, Montana, I got into the extra caboose for a more comfortable ride. Between Libby and Whitefish, there was an eleven-mile tunnel. It was pitch dark in the tunnel, and I made the mistake of turning the light on. The crew came in from the other caboose. They were scared about what might be going on, but when they found it was just me, they were kind and allowed me to stay in the caboose. We soon arrived at the next stop, Whitefish. I hitchhiked to West Glacier and went into the park. I had decided I was going to hike over Gunsight Pass. It was early enough in the season, around June, that the crews were still shoveling the trails that crossed the glaciers. I spent a couple of nights camping, snoozing in a sleeping bag under the moon the first night. The mountain goats were skipping around, and it felt like they were jumping over me. The next day one of the whistling marmots came up to me. I was lying in the sun with my boots off and let it lick the sweat off of my bare feet—until it started nibbling. After a few days of fasting and praying, I returned to the railroad yard and found there were no empty boxcars returning. I saw a boxcar that had plywood up the side full of wheat that had been augured into it, going to market. I climbed up over the plywood and found that the door was partially opened, so I slid up into the car to discover it had seven feet of wheat in it. It was the nicest freight ride I ever had. The wheat formed to my body and the weight of the grain kept the car from jumping around. In later years, I used that knowledge when we were working with different wheelchair seating cushions that were built to distribute weight.

I considered our group, tongue in cheek, to be "Hobos for Jesus." We purposefully went out of our way not to label ourselves. In the scriptures, the believers were first called Christians in Antioch, not Mennonites, Lutherans, Calvinists, Wesleyans, or any other name of a man. These were great men of God, but we are not called to follow them but rather to see them as examples of how they followed Christ. In I Corinthians 11:1, Paul tells us that we are to, "Be ye followers of me, even as I also am of Christ." We were Christ followers and referred to each other as brothers and sisters in the Lord. Avoiding a label was important to us. It was hard to call ourselves the church since we were not like any traditional church that we knew in any sense.

During Thanksgiving of 1974, our group was staying in El Paso, Texas. A few of us went across the border and camped just outside Ciudad, Juarez. We would go to the public parks and do street evangelism. We spent our days there, carrying our Bibles, and looking for those who wanted to hear about Jesus. There was a young girl who had accepted the Lord. Because of the strong Catholic tradition of her grandparents, they felt threatened by us and called the police. The police, thinking they'd kill two birds with one stone, figured they'd chase us back across the border while extorting money from us. They rounded up a couple of us and took us to the police station. The police told us they were going to take us across the bridge and escort us out of Mexico into El Paso. What they didn't count on was that when they turned us back over to the arresting officers, they refused to take us to the border without taking our money.

I was put in a holding cell with seven other inmates. There was a hole in the floor for a toilet and a tin can that had some food leftover from breakfast. The inmates offered what was left in the can to me, saying it was "atole." Knowing next to no Spanish I thought they were trying to say toilet. Atole is actually watered-down oatmeal. The officers came back a half-hour later, giving me time to become pretty scared. They came back to the cell and through the bars, showed me a letter they wanted me to sign before they could release me. I had about $83.00, and they conveniently gave me a fine of $80.00. I was told I had to sign this letter, which stated I was teaching things that were unlawful to teach and told me if I refused to sign it, they'd transfer me to the Chihuahua State Penitentiary. I'm sure they had done this many times and everyone gladly forfeited the money. As a conscientious Christian, I saw it as an act of denying Jesus if I paid a bribe or did anything corrupt, so I refused. I laughed at them when they showed me the letter, thinking it was a bluff. Because the officers had to save face, within an hour, I was in the nearby Chihuahua State Penitentiary in a cellblock with sixty other inmates.

Normally they would put people in the city jail, but I learned that the condition of the jail was so bad at the time that, instead, they would put Americans in the penitentiary in Juarez so the American consulate would not see how bad the city jail really was. This penitentiary was for those serving less than five-year sentences. The main penitentiary was 200 miles away and in the City of Chihuahua. Fortunately, they let me keep my Bible, and I had $3.00 left. Meals consisted of a bowl of oatmeal gruel (watered-down oatmeal, sugar, and cinnamon) for breakfast and a bowl of pinto beans for lunch and dinner.

Only once did I get boiled potatoes. The meal always came with a piece of bread. You could buy tortillas in the courtyard, as well as other snacks. The prison staff basically let the inmates run the prison. First, I was taken to the lead prisoner so he could interview me. They hoped I would give them my family's contact information so they could contact them, using a crooked Mexican lawyer. Their plan was to extort money from families, claiming they could help get me released if money was sent to them. I refused to tell them and they left me alone. When they learned I had stood up to the police corruption, they respected me for not being fearful.

Half of the inmates paid the warden so they could hang blankets from 2'x 2' frames in order to have some privacy. The rest slept on the concrete floor. It was late November, and the nights were very cold, being at almost 4,000 feet elevation. Within three days, the American consulate came. It still took a few more days to get released, so I ended up spending a week in the prison. I was able to use that time to share the gospel with the inmates in my cell, as well as in the courtyard with inmates from other cellblocks. These prisoners included some Americans, one Canadian, and a man from England. Four U.S. army soldiers from Ft. Bliss were also being held. Drugs had been planted on them so the police could confiscate their new 1975 Pontiac. Some years before, Richard Nixon had passed a law that Americans could not get bailed out of foreign prisons if they were being held on drug charges.

There was one inmate who had been in for a few years who was from Black Harlem. He walked out of a bar late at night and got mugged. He beat up all three of the muggers, putting one of them in the hospital. His release time was coming up, but they wouldn't release him until he paid the hospital bill of the guy he beat up. A kind Baptist pastor from El Paso was working to help him. Following Paul's example, we shared the Good News in whatever situation we ended up. In Philippians 4:12, Paul states, "I know both how to be abased, and I know how to abound: everywhere and in all things I am instructed both to be full and to be hungry, both to abound and to suffer need." When I was released I was given the envelope with my ID and my original $80.00.

In the summer of 1975, we decided to reach out to the Rainbow Family. The Rainbow Family was a group that began after Woodstock and had a gathering every summer in the United States, as well as in other countries. Most participants were hippies and drug users. Nudity, free sex, and other destructive practices were encouraged. That year, the annual gathering was being held in Arkansas in a national park on the Buffalo River. A few brothers and I went to Arkansas in order to scout out locations and resources for the rest of the group. We wanted to reach out and share Jesus with the young people that would be flooding this area. We went to Fayetteville, Arkansas, and I went to the local food coop to buy some food. I noticed a man who had the appearance of one who bore witness that he was a man of God. It turned out to be Marvin Miller, a gentleman who had left the Amish in the late '60s and moved his family to British Honduras, now Belize. In the early '70s he moved back to the United States and settled in Arkansas. We walked up to him, observing his bib overalls and long, bushy beard. He looked like one of the Plain people, and we started talking as he was walked into the same store. We wanted to learn more about where he was with his walk with the Lord and told him we were camping at the park. We used the term "the brethren" and that was enough: he knew we were believers. Thirty minutes later, he showed up at the park and invited us to his farm, which was less than an hour away. He, with his wife and five kids, shared acreage with his brother's family. Marvin was fascinated that we were reaching out to people for Jesus. Later that day, we hitchhiked out to his farm, and they received us like angels. They "killed the fatted calf," served homemade strawberry juice, and sat with us in the shade of the tree to eat. We felt like we were in the middle of an Old Testament story.

Marvin Miller introduced us to a book called *Martyrs Mirror* by Thieleman J. van Braght. This book contained graphic accounts of Christians who had become martyrs because of their faith in the gospel of Jesus Christ. Common themes encouraged us to love our enemies and return good for evil. It called believers to follow Jesus in all areas of life, even unto death. Come what may, true Christian commitment demands supreme discipleship and steadfast adherence to the teachings modeled by Jesus and his apostles. This book was written and published in 1659 to strengthen the faith of his fellow believers. In 1886, it was translated into English to challenge new generations of Christians in North America. Marvin also introduced us to the writings of Menno Simons.

Marvin was raised Old Order Amish. Like us, they were the nonconformists, non-resistant people of their time and culture. Their religious beliefs were also similar to ours. Marvin had left all for Jesus, something we deeply believed in and lived out.

Soon after, the rest of our group arrived and we went to the Rainbow Gathering. Unfortunately, they happily invited us in but few received our message. Instead, they encouraged us to participate in their drugs. When we stayed at the Rainbow gathering, we didn't want to camp with them. They always stayed in the woods, and because of their drug use and nudity, we stayed separate from them. One of my old friends, Mike Kovak, was at this gathering. Mike was the person with whom I had been traveling when I found the ministry on the streets of Berkeley four years before. When we were leaving the valley, we saw each other and just walked side by side, talking. Mike is still very close to my family, including my brothers. He writes music and performs Bluegrass with a group called Windfall. Running into him was another example of how many times in my life my relationships have been cyclical. Just because you move away or go down different paths does not mean the relationship has ended or you'll never see that person again.

After the Rainbow gathering ended, we continued to camp on Marvin's farm for a long time. This was the beginning of a lifelong friendship. Throughout my life, many seemingly random, unconnected events have been illuminated as divine appointments—ones that have resulted in relationships, which have come into play years later.

For instance, when I lived with the Joe Miller family, I found out Joe was part of that same movement Marvin Miller's family was involved with while in Belize. These connections were a blessing from the Lord on my life and my ministry and continue to this day. I have stayed in touch with Marvin's oldest daughter, Hope, who with her husband Ray, has adopted many children with disabilities.

In the summer of 1976, we went to Montreal for the Olympics. We found an old, run- down apartment building owned by Joe Dale. He was in poor health and had let his six-story apartment building with twenty-four units deteriorate.

He let us have two apartments in exchange for us providing maintenance and upkeep to the building.

I spent some time in Montreal during the Olympics but mainly stayed in Washington, D.C. during this time. This was when the Treasures of King Tutankhamen started its six-city tour, and millions came to see it from across the United States. When I was nine years old, my parents had taken my brothers and me to see the King Tut treasure display at the Los Angeles museum in November 1962, so I just had to see this too.

We were getting free rent on a two-unit townhouse in exchange for some remodeling just ten blocks from the Smithsonian. The first time I saw the exhibit, I only had a thirty-five minute wait, but within a couple of days, the line stretched for a few blocks, taking hours for people to get in. Around this time, some of the sisters in the ministry found a couple of heavy wool coats, which had been used by the White House guards in a thrift store in D.C. They didn't have the fancy buttons to replace lost ones, so they sewed some simple buttons on them and gave me one. I was ready to hitchhike up to Montreal with Brother Enoch.

We decided to visit the Hutterian Society of Brethren in Rifton, New York. This is the same group Jacob Maendel had spent time with. About dark, we were at a rest area on the New York thruway, and someone walking back to his car asked us if we wanted a ride to North Poughkeepsie. We accepted and when we arrived, it was late and cold, so he let us stay at the housing co-op where he had a room. We slept in the common living room on the couches. In the morning, we started talking to one of the guys who lived there, and we told him we were going to the Society of Brothers in Rifton. He said, "I'm an insurance adjuster and my first stop is at the Society of Brothers because of a small fire they had in their carpentry shop." We arrived and they welcomed us, but they didn't quite know what to do with us as we were walking in the 16th-century Hutterite lifestyle more accurately than they were.

At this time the Society was building high-quality wooden toys under the name Community Playthings. Today, they build Rifton Equipment for children with disabilities. We have refurbished much of their therapy equipment and shipped them internationally over the years. On a few occasions, they have donated to us returned equipment. Here was another example of a relationship, which has stretched into the future, benefitting our wheelchair ministry. The family we stayed with was in tears when we told them about the miracle of how we got there. They had joined the Bruderhof, wanting a closer walk with the Lord and felt like there was something missing. They were impressed with our childlike faith.

After a few days with them, we hitchhiked to the freight yard in St Albans, Vermont, where we climbed into an empty gondola freight car bound for Montreal. Because Canada did not like vagrants coming in from the States with no money, we entered in this way so as not to give the Canadian immigration officials a chance to turn us away. In the open gondola, with the temperature hovering around zero degrees Fahrenheit, it was the coldest night I have ever spent outdoors, and I do believe we could have froze to death. Because the gondolas are open at the top, the wind kicked around the snow that was already in the car. We had pretty good sleeping bags, but I was wearing tennis shoes. I took them off and slept with them to try to keep them warm so that in the morning, I'd have warm shoes to put on. Even though it was hovering around zero, the wind chill probably brought the temperature down another ten or twenty degrees. I have to admit that freezing to death did cross my mind. When we arrived, we jumped off the train into a snow bank before getting into the train yard. We walked into a corner store to warm up before walking to the house. We were experts at being homeless and by this time, the Brothers knew where to get food for free. Some of our favorites included flour from the Robin Hood Flour Mill, ice cream from the ice cream factory, cheese from the gourmet cheese factory, and the steak house for trimmings of meat. We had enough to eat.

One of our favorites was a Caribbean store that set out all kinds of tropical fruit and vegetables. We made homemade flour tortillas and steak burritos with homemade hot sauce regularly. I put on fifteen pounds that winter, mainly because we had so much maple walnut and chocolate ice cream. We learned to make hot chocolate out of the chocolate ice cream. It was a very cold winter, and one day it even reached forty-four degrees below zero. This was an amazing season, and I was blessed with time to stay in one place for a couple of months.

I usually never stayed places longer than two weeks during my seven years with the group.

What I had joined was a traveling evangelistic ministry. Because of the leader's exclusive self-righteousness, over the years, he gradually led us into becoming less accepting, less tolerant of others, and required that we looked down on others who weren't as sold-out as we were. We became judgmental and self-righteous. Eventually, we no longer considered ourselves a ministry. Instead, we started calling ourselves The Church. We became cultish. What started as a movement of God, a wonderful stepping-stone out of unbelief into belief, but it turned into a snare. If you didn't believe exactly what we believed, you were considered a backslider. The other members shunned anyone who disagreed or left the group. I couldn't advance in the leadership of the group because I wasn't toeing that self-righteous line.

God meets people where they are. I didn't need to go and find a local church, a Bible study, or a workshop. I needed discipleship and teaching. I needed to be surrounded by other young believers who were totally sold out, seeking to learn and grow. Unfortunately, we weren't getting the well-balanced teaching we needed. Our group had provided so much for me for a long time, but it was a mixed blessing because the teaching wasn't well balanced. When Jim Roberts became abusive and controlling, it turned out that what he really wanted was to control everyone's life. He told us that we were The Church and if you left the ministry, you were leaving God. What started out so well but eventually sank into spiritual abuse.

Leaders can use their authority to control people. Religion has been used to control and manipulate others since biblical times. Jesus hung out with the sinners and the poor, not the religious leaders of the time. In fact, Jesus was outwardly critical of the manipulative, greedy actions of the Pharisees. He was so hated and feared by the Pharisees because of his truth-telling that it resulted in a plan to kill him. I wanted to spend my life helping the poor and disabled. To me, this was and is my way of following the Lord's command, "…Thou shalt love thy neighbour as thyself." (Matthew 22: 39b) This ministry could have remained a powerful stepping-stone out of drugs for many. One of my friends, Jim Guerra, wrote a book called *From Deans List to Dumpsters*. Jim has gone on to write and talk about this spiritual abuse.

Philip Haney was another one of those young people who were completely sold out for the Lord. In November 1975, I met Philip in Davis, California. Philip was majoring in entomology at the University of California at Davis. The traveling ministry often went to different universities and colleges to witness and recruit. We traveled to Davis with quite a few of the brothers and sisters. We spoke in the park or wherever we could find people who wanted to listen. Philip met one of the brothers, Barry, who shared the gospel with him for the first time in his life. For Philip, that relationship with the Lord continues to this day.

Philip had met his wife, Francesca, at Davis where they were both renting rooms from a Russian woman who worked at the university. They were married and together when they first met us. Within a month, they both quit school and joined the ministry. In Luke, the Lord teaches us to forsake all for the sake of the gospel, and the ministry took it literally. Philip and Francesca adopted our beliefs immediately.

I was one of the people who had been in the group for a long time. We called each other older and younger brothers, depending on how long we'd been with the ministry. We believed in giving, selling, or throwing away everything we owned—absolutely everything. I helped Philip and Francesca through this, a traumatizing process for almost everyone. The only thing we kept was their car, which we pulled into use for the ministry.

Francesca had been married before when she was much younger. She grew up in a horrendously abusive home, perpetrated by her father. In her late teens, she left, taking an offer of marriage as a means of escape. She didn't know what it was to be in a normal relationship and that first marriage ended. When Philip met her, they fell in love and got married. The group told them the marriage was adulterous since she had been married before and required them to separate. They were even put into different traveling groups so they were rarely able to see each other.

I tried to be very kind. I wasn't legalistic, judgmental, or self-righteous, like many of the others, especially the leaders. I tried to support them, and we were able to develop deep friendships. In testimony to our deep friendship, Philip, Francesca, Sandy, and I have remained very close to this day.

We all went through spiritual abuse. The more independent and creative you were, the more trouble you usually had. The leaders were so strict and legalistic that there was absolutely no discussion about the decisions they made. You had to conform, or they would leave you or send you someplace where you'd be abandoned.

Francesca walked away from it first. She went through a lot more than Philip did. She had lost a baby along the way, and Philip was never told about it. She hemorrhaged and almost died while miscarrying the baby. Francesca and Philip rarely saw each other, and when they did, they weren't allowed to be alone together.

During this time, I had become friends with Philip since we were in the same camp. For a few years, we went from place to place, sharing the word of God and fellowshipping. We were both pretty bad in that we broke many of the rules the leaders tried to enforce. For instance, both of us like to read and learn. We "erred" by reading about history, books like *Pilgrim's Progress*. We weren't supposed to read anything except for the Bible. However, we both felt that if we wanted to work and connect with people, we needed to learn and grow in knowledge and wisdom. I was naturally good at connecting with people and quickly developing relationships. I liked being around people, and they usually liked being around me. However, when it came to organization, Philip was and is extremely talented. Being a scientist, he was able to take those "big ideas" and figure out how to bring them to fruition. He understood my ideas, organized them, and communicated them well. We made a good team.

At one point, Philip and I were in Immokalee, Florida, working with the migrant workers. We'd purposefully go where people were seeking. Most of those we encountered were there illegally from Mexico, but there were also some legal citizens who were very poor. A Mennonite man who was responsible for a center in town let us use it to witness. We worked in the fields with the migrant workers and while working alongside them we shared the gospel. We were much more effective when we worked with people and were not afraid of getting our hands dirty. We lived one day at a time and made no promises to anyone; always willing to go where we felt the Lord was leading.

Here in the United States, most of us have a lot of padding between living well and struggling. We have health insurance, house insurance, vehicle insurance, welfare, government programs, and other safety nets. The very poor or illegal citizens in the United States and especially the poor in developing countries don't have those man-made securities and have to rely on God for their daily provisions. Their faith is being built daily as they experience, all too vividly, the spiritual battle raging around them. They see God's work in their lives every day, as well as the miracles he gifts them with. Through my time working with them, I've learned so much about depending on God for all things, every day. Their obedience and faith are often based on their previous experiences with the Lord. When we depend on the Lord rather than man or money for our security, we will experience true faith.

Philip left the group. This was hard for all of us, including him. In spite of the problems with the group's abusive leadership, we had a deep friendship with each other. We'd been through a lot and had gained many wonderful insights about truths in the Bible. Throughout our travels, we experienced, first hand, God's intervention and provision. Everyone who met the Lord and was truly Spirit-filled eventually left the group. Philip related this ministry experience to his first profession in entomology. As with planting a seed in a hot box, when the seeds germinate, they do fine until they bump into the glass. They're still getting light, but they come to a point where if they stay in there, they become deformed and don't grow the way they were supposed to. But if transplanted out of it, they will grow like they were meant to.

By leaving the group, we were able to grow and serve the Lord without man-made rules and restrictions. Give permission to the Lord to provide the circumstances and situations that will help you grow to be the person He created you to be. "And he shall be like a tree planted by the rivers of water, that bringeth forth his fruit in his season; his leaf also shall not wither; and whatsoever he doeth shall prosper." (Psalm 1:3)

Philip went back to his past life and found it to be extremely hard. He had been gone for three and a half years and had not once returned home. He found that the things he'd left behind had changed. Everyone else in his life had moved on, and he didn't know where Francesca was located. He eventually found her, and they resumed their marriage. It was very difficult for them to regain normalcy, but they did and still serve the Lord to this day. One of those areas of service involved the ministry. In the mid-1990s, a group of parents formed a support group, The Roberts Parents Group. This group consisted of families that had children who disappeared within the group. Francesca and Philip reached out to them and the group adopted them. They helped the families by providing information and insights into the ministry and became a great source of inspiration. This group is still operating today.

Meanwhile, I started the process of leaving the ministry, and we lost track of one another. Over the years, we started seeking each other. I reconnected with Philip in 1982 when I was in Los Angeles after I had returned from Belize. I went to visit him in Ventura, where he was working on biological control of insects in the citrus industry. After that, we saw each other when we could as we moved around the country. I visited them when they moved to Auburn, Georgia, where Philip was pursuing his doctorate. Philip was also a part of the group the ABC Network flew to New York in 1999. Diane Sawyer did a *Primetime* investigation about the traveling group, using the label "The Brethren." This documentary aired on April 5th and included families who had lost their children to the cult. Philip, Francesca, Sandy, Stan Avery (another previous member), and I were part of the story. Diane Sawyer didn't get the response she expected from us, as we weren't willing to totally slam the group but instead we shared the good with the bad. Since we've reconnected, we've never lost contact again. They have even gone on wheelchair trips with us. Stan works in ministry, mainly in India.

Many in the group didn't fare so well. Social adjustment issues were prevalent. When leaving the group, it wasn't about rejecting the Lord but about trying to re-enter society and function. It's tricky trying to describe this. We had such a mixture of real, genuine, spectacular experiences—miracles— and incredible events, which only the Lord could have made happen. However, other experiences we faced within the group were traumatizing and damaging.

Some of the people who left the group became recluses or remained dysfunctional. Others would get worse, meaning more legalistic, than the original leaders of the group. Occasionally, Philip and I still meet people who remained in the group, and it feels like spiritual warfare. They typically condemn us. When Philip had this experience, what struck him was that all of these years later, they were exactly where they had been, spiritually, when we left the group. It hit home, as he realized just how toxic that environment had been.

Jim Roberts died in December 2015, but the group still exists. Families are still searching for children who disappeared with the group years ago. Fortunately, most of the members have at least reconnected with their loved ones. I just learned of someone who visited his dying mother after many years away, and it wasn't until his third visit that she realized it was the son that had left her so many years before.

Our experiences in the ministry gave us a unique perspective in life. We're capable of managing with very little. We learned to live on less than a dollar a day, and we made almost everything we used, including sleeping bags, tents, clothes, and shoes. We knew how to live outside in sub-zero weather and how to find shelter without any money. Philip reflected on this and applied it to my life when he said, "To this day, Mark sinks everything into his ministry—it all goes to wheelchairs for people. He has no pretense and gives his all to the Lord." Being in the group destroyed any pretense: we got down to who we really were. Many of us became true friends and it's why we're still friends. We don't regret it, although we remain sad about many of the things that happened.

Philip and I also learned about spiritual warfare in the group. It's hard to apply what we learned in more peaceful times, but now it's coming to the forefront again as we see our country changing. Christians need to be in the Word daily and in deep prayer in order to combat the many violent forces, which are at work in the United States. God is in control and is more powerful than the enemy. As His people, it is our responsibility to pray and speak out for Him in love and as peacemakers.

Philip has proven his integrity and compassion many times over the years. At one point, an Israeli "cowboy" was bringing Quarter Horses into the United States and Philip worked with him. From then on, he wanted to travel to Israel one day and visit the cowboy. On a wheelchair distribution trip with Hope Haven International in 2003, his dream came true, and we were able to visit these stables overlooking the Sea of Galilee. The entire distribution team was able to ride Quarter Horses in the hills overlooking the Sea of Galilee, an incredible experience.

CHAPTER 8

RIPENING

'm sure I should have been diagnosed with some form of attention deficit disorder. Looking back, though, I wonder if I had been diagnosed, would it have squashed my creativity? My brother Chad, who is one year younger than me, was eventually diagnosed with dyslexia. To this day, Chad can't read well but is incredibly creative. He's mechanically gifted and his people skills are amazing. He's traveled all over the world and has been a blessing to so many. God can use anyone, no matter his or her ability or disability. Chad is gifted with teaching and has trained many youth to be tradesmen. His story demonstrates how we need to be open to His calling and know Him well so we can discern His voice from the racket of the world.

Learning different languages has always interested me. After my stay in the Mexican prison, I studied Spanish. I had always had the desire to learn Spanish, but I didn't like the classroom environment—it didn't work for me.

In the winter of 1976–1977, while in Montreal, Quebec, I decided to learn French too. One of the brothers in the group, Guiton, spent an hour every day with me. I studied French, his native language, and would help him with his English. I procured a French New Testament and read it alongside the English translation. Eventually, I reached a place where I could understand and read French pretty well.

Within a year, I was living near the Pennsylvania Dutch and decided to learn German. From 1978 to 1983, I lived with people who spoke Pennsylvania Dutch (German), High German, Swiss German, and Low German. I ended up learning a smattering of it all, but the Pennsylvania Dutch was prevalent. The fact that I became somewhat fluent in even one of these proved to me that I could learn, even though my experience in formal schooling had told me I couldn't.

Later, when in Belize, I had to learn Belizean Creole (pidgin English). It didn't take long for me to understand and speak it because, in northern Belize, the native Creole could understand American English, but the Mopan and Kekchi Mayans in the Southern part of Belize couldn't, and I needed to communicate with them. Since Creole was their second language, after I learned it, I was able to communicate. Eventually, I learned some phrases in Kekchi and Mopan from church, the Bible, and songbooks, which proved useful.

Although I am fairly fluent when communicating in Spanish, apparently it's not perfect. In 1992, I was in the Presidential Palace with Magna de Serrano, the first Lady of Guatemala, discussing plans to bring more wheelchairs and doing a wheelchair delivery with Joni Eareckson Tada, an inspirational speaker and author. In the middle of our meeting, she started to chuckle. When I asked what was funny, she said I was speaking Spanish with a Mayan Campesino accent. I had learned most of my Spanish from Mayans, whose second language is Spanish. She had probably never heard a blue-eyed gringo speak like a Mayan hillbilly. This meeting occurred not too many years after, while at a Christian conference before being the first lady, she had met Joni. At this time, we hoped to have Joni come down during a wheelchair delivery. I was on staff then with Joni and Friends and was the Program Director for Wheels for the World. Soon after our meeting, there was a coup, and the Serranos went into exile in Panama.

By December 1977, one of the other brothers and I were questioning the leadership in the ministry, and when comparing notes, determined the group was more about the leader maintaining control than serving Jesus anymore. My exit strategy was to go to Puerto Rico and the Caribbean and do evangelism there. We saved money doing migrant farm work in the Everglades. We had just about enough money when one of the brothers got arrested for vagrancy in one of the northeastern states, so we sent the money to bail him out. Anxious to get out, Brother Enoch and I finally earned enough money doing fieldwork for both of us to purchase one-way tickets to Puerto Rico for $100 each, leaving the States with just $100 in cash between us. When we arrived, we camped on the beaches in hammocks we strung up and moved around the country. I used the little bit of Spanish I had learned during my time in the Chihuahua State Penitentiary in Juarez, Mexico, so I was able to communicate—somewhat. Brian had about as much Spanish as I did, so we managed. Since Puerto Rico was a U.S. territory, there were many people who spoke English.

We didn't formally leave The Assembly, but we just never went back. In San Juan, we ended up connecting with Jesus freak colleagues who called themselves La Catacombas in reference to the early Christians of Rome who had to hide in the Catacombs to avoid persecution. This was an independent group, homegrown in Puerto Rico, which did street evangelism. In San Juan, we also met some of the Children of God members. This was a group that started during the Jesus Movement but their founder and leader, David Berg, led many of them into terrible immorality, including pedophilia and prostitution. One of the friends I was traveling with had come out of the background of witchcraft before becoming a Christian. He had been the head of a coven in Tulsa, Oklahoma. He knew a lot about witchcraft, demon possession, and familiar spirits. We were able to talk to the local leadership and advised them that what they were involved in was nothing short of witchcraft. Unfortunately, they were not open to the truth and we were shown the door.

Puerto Rico was like a foreign country, and there again, we learned to have total dependence on God. We had no backup resources and knew no one in the country. Each day, we woke up, prayed, and faced the day with expectancy for a chance to share the gospel. We relied on Him for opportunities to share and for our basic needs. Resources were scarce, but we always had what we needed. I was agile enough to shimmy up the many coconut trees on public land to get coconuts to drink and eat. At one point, we could find no place to camp, so we hung our hammocks in the banyan trees, provided of course by our Lord. Finding trees on a beach to string up the hammocks was not a problem, but in an urban area, you did not want to be at ground level for all to see. The banyan tree allowed us to sleep twenty-five feet in the air.

We decided to find work in the pineapple fields. We showed up at the employment office hoping to get sent to a job site. The director of the employment office had never seen white mainlanders looking to do migrant work. He was convinced we were sent by the U.S. Department of Labor to investigate the corruption that was widespread in government jobs in Puerto Rico. He sat us down in his office and started crying and pleading for us not take his job. No amount of persuading would convince him that we really just wanted to work in the fields. We never did get a job, so we hitchhiked west to Rincon. Later, we found work with a Christian couple painting their house and doing landscape work at the Presbyterian church they attended.

After nearly two months in Puerto Rico, we went to the Virgin Islands, and I ended up getting a job with a painting contractor. We had a place on the beach near the airport where we camped in our hammocks, stringing a tent fly over them to keep us dry in the rain. We used a locker at the airport for twenty-five cents a day to store our backpacks and gear. We were near the capital, Charlotte Amalie, and would go into town to work. Eventually, we made friends with members of The Shiloh Ministries, another fringe Jesus Movement group. This was a ministry to which a lot of young people had flocked. All of their members had full-time jobs and turned over their entire paychecks to the leaders. Unfortunately, this led the way to abuse, also.

We stayed with them for a few days and went to church with them. Unfortunately, the local leader only wanted to talk about us joining them and turning over our paychecks. It seems to me the biggest snare that destroys these types of ministries involves the lack of accountability. A lot of young, novice leaders were put into these positions, and they often fell quickly into sin because of power and pride. Paul talks about the concerns of having a young believer in a power position of leadership. "This is a true saying, if a man desire the office of a bishop, he desireth a good work. Not a novice, lest being lifted up with pride he fall into the condemnation of the devil." (1 Timothy 3: 1, 6)

In April, I left the Virgin Islands after three months in the Caribbean and hopped on a flight back to Puerto Rico where I could find inexpensive night flights to the Newark, New Jersey area. After landing in Newark, I hitchhiked to a community in Alliance, Ohio, called Fairmount Fellowship. It was April of 1978 when I ended up in Ohio with my friend Jacob Maendel, who led Fairmount Fellowship. When Jacob had left the Hutterites for the second time, he moved to Stark County, Ohio and bought an old county children's home. This home became a safe haven for a lot of people from different Jesus Movement ministries who were disillusioned. At that time, there were at least seven former members from my old traveling ministry living there, including Andrew and Deborah Neal, Chuck and Kathy Wimberley, Tom and Julie McCune, and Brian Walsh.

Fairmount was a community of people that lived and worked together, sharing all they had. This was another example of how God continued to connect me with people who would become instrumental in helping others. Throughout the years, our work has often been tied together. Jacob was in the salvage industry and helped get us to find tools, which we used in our wheelchair refurbishing and production at sites in Iowa, South Dakota, and Guatemala. Years later, following in his grandfather's footsteps, his grandson Dana, with his wife Rosa, helped establish the Youth With a Mission base in Antigua, Guatemala. Ten years later, Dana's father and mother, Sam and Annie, moved to Guatemala to live and volunteer for Hope Haven.

In mid-April, a former Amish man, Levi Mast, came to visit Fairmount Fellowship. After meeting with me, Levi offered me a job in Millersburg, Ohio as his tender. He was a cement mason and block layer in his community. I went to work for him and lived with them as I was still in transition after leaving the traveling ministry. Levi was loosely connected to the group of ex-Amish remnants in Ohio, Pennsylvania, Tennessee, and Indiana of the Old Order Plain People. During that time a revival was going on with the Old Order communities that focused on questioning their traditions. I ended up visiting a lot of those disgruntled souls who were trying to sort out what was a tradition of man and what was a commandment of God. Reformation involved taking church history and the traditions of man and determining what needed to be reformed. In contrast, the Anabaptists and the Jesus Movement believed in tossing out all of the church rituals and traditions and starting over by going to the source, specifically the Gospels and the book of Acts. We were a novelty to each other and yet similar in our quest. The interesting thing was that most of these people weren't ready to throw away their good traditions. They saw the downside of being modern and what it did to the family. Most chose to keep the horse and buggy, daily devotions, and the commitment to hard work through farming. They would go on to start their own communities outside of the Old Order communities.

Levi introduced me to the community in Lobelville, Tennessee. I got to know some of the folks in this group who were made up of Old Order Amish, Old Order Mennonites, and German Baptists. I was attracted to this group and learned so much from them. In spite of my learning disability, I had a great love of knowledge and history and immersed myself in reading and learning. This community provided a setting where I could learn infinitely better than in a classroom environment.

During the daytime, I helped with farm work, carpentry, logging, and in the sawmill. We spent a lot of time talking about what the Bible teaches and 16th century Anabaptist history. They all had *The Martyrs Mirror* and the writings of Menno Simons and Dietrick Philips, but they also had books by John Bunyan and other old writers. I read the Martin Luther German Bible in the old script just to learn German.

During my time in the traveling ministry, I had spent a lot of hours in university and public libraries, fascinated with church history. Much of my study had focused on first and 16th century Christianity. The book of Acts and the Gospels fed my zeal for God. Looking back, I was probably over-legalistic, but it turned out to be a good thing at the time. I devoured Foxe's *Book of Martyrs* and felt more in common with the Anabaptists than the mainstream reformers, those who brought about the Protestant movement. My faith convinced me that it was right not to just reform but to reject the Roman Church's man-made traditions. I embraced early Christian beliefs and practices, which were based on the teachings of Jesus and the apostles from the Gospels and the book of Acts.

By this time, I was with the Amish descendants, the Anabaptists. There were three original branches of the Plain People, including the Hutterites, the Mennonites, and the Amish. The Amish didn't know what to think of me, since I knew more about their history and faith traditions than the vast majority of them. I looked like them with my long beard and way of dress. At that time, I was very unique because I was an outsider who was accepted into this closed community and considered part of the family. For about three years, from 1978 into 1980, I lived and worked with them.

I was living with the Simon Beachy family when my brother, David, stopped by for a few days to visit. I didn't know this at the time, but he was running a load of marijuana from Florida to Madison, Wisconsin, making himself some money by filling in for a friend who usually made the run. Forty years later, David confided in me. During that visit, he had 310 pounds of pot in the trunk of his Mazda.

David had been working by selling advertisements for a rock and roll magazine in the Midwest. He was around a lot of drugs, especially cocaine, and soon acquired a serious drug habit. What it took was for his life to be threatened for him to realize he needed to get out of Wisconsin and away from the people with whom he was involved. In 1983, he moved out to California and joined Denny, who had just joined AA (Alcoholics Anonymous) and had become sober. They were both staying at my mom's apartment in Torrance, California. One day, David, who had just bought some heroin, went into her bathroom to shoot up. Denny intervened and they both knelt down in front of the toilet and prayed as they flushed it down. They have remained sober and clean ever since.

Lobelville was a very unique community. The two leaders were Paul Lavey, who came from the Old Order German Baptists, and Henry Mast, who came from the Old Order Amish in Iowa. Shortly after being established in Tennessee, a few other families that had come from the Delaware Amish, including the Simon Beachy and Joe Beachy families, joined them. Simon established himself as the main preacher in the community. Another family joined them when Joe J. Miller moved his family from southern Indiana. During my time in Tennessee, I lived with all three of these families, and they made me feel like one of the sons.

While I was staying with the Miller family, a young man joined us by the name of John Stoll. In Hickman County, John and I helped Joe Miller build his homestead in Cane Creek, a satellite community of the Russell Creek original settlement, while living in the loft of his barn. I learned a lot from Joe Miller, especially how to work with a team of horses. One time, we were pulling some logs up an embankment, and he was letting me handle the horse. He said something that stuck with me. We were using just one horse at a time and had moved most of the logs up the embankment. Looking at the last log, I said, "Well should I hitch it up?"

He explained, "No, it's too big. If the horse tries to pull it up and it can't, you could ruin him. In the future, whenever it comes to something big, it might just balk and think it can't do it. You don't want to discourage him with failure by making it too hard for him."

This was a good life lesson. It's easy for us to set others up to fail by making impossible demands or having irrational expectations—in work, relationships, and spiritually. Jesus reprimanded the Pharisees in Matthew 23:4, "For they bind heavy burdens and grievous to be borne, and lay them on men's shoulders; but they themselves will not move them with one of their fingers." In Matthew 11:28, Jesus calls us, "Come unto me, all ye that labour and are heavy laden, and I will give you rest."

In the spring of 1978, it rained hard one night, and there was a tragic flood. John and I looked out from the loft in the barn and realized we were in the middle of three feet of water. It was still dark, but we had to go down and save the livestock. We took the cow to dry land. We knew the horse had just had a foal, not even a week old. The colt was struggling to keep its head above water, and we were afraid the water was going to continue to rise. Between the two of us, we took the colt up the ladder into the loft so it wouldn't drown. We soon realized the foal wanted to nurse and was crying for its mother. I got a bucket and milked the mare and was able to give the foal some milk. We assumed that the water would stay up for a long time, but fortunately, it went down within a half a day. Probably the worst damage that the flood caused was to the cabin. We had been working on disassembling a one-hundred-year-old cabin, which was made out of oak and poplar. The main beams were oak and the rest was poplar.

We treated it more like a barn raising, as the whole community helped pull it apart and numbered every part so that we could reassemble it somewhere else.

While I had been helping them take it apart, I was up on the roof removing sheeting when I stepped onto the ceiling and fell through. My Amish friends thought I'd probably broken my neck. They called down, and I was so embarrassed that all I could do was laugh while lying on the main floor of the house. By the time of the flood, every log was numbered and neatly organized, but the waters washed all the logs down Cane Creek, never to be seen again.

Later, in 1981, John and I took buses across Mexico to Belize. At this time, Mexico was one of the cheapest countries in which to travel. We had a missionary friend who boasted he could drive from Brownsville, Texas to the Belize border for five dollars with his diesel VW Rabbit. At that time, diesel was only nineteen cents a gallon. I couldn't believe the Mexico City subway cost only about four cents to go anywhere. We stopped at the Mayan ruins of Palenque for a few days. We were backpacking and in those days, they had thatched huts where the backpackers could put up their hammocks. It was a wonderful trip, giving me yet another opportunity to connect with a dear friend.

In the fall of 1978, after working and living with the Levi Mast family in Ohio, I decided to go out to Cape Cod to visit Andrew and Deborah Neal. They had moved back to Cape Cod in order to return to where Andrew was originally from. While hitchhiking on I-80, I ended up getting a ride with a Mennonite man who happened to be a friend of Levi's. He was going to Pennsylvania and took me to the home of Eli Miller whom I had met the summer before. I ended up spending the whole winter with the Eli Miller family, a family that consisted of two daughters and a son, Mark, who became a good friend. I traveled with Eli to Pennsylvania, Indiana, and Tennessee to meet other like-minded, born-again Amish.

Eli was raised Old Order Amish and was walking close to the Bible. Eli and his wife took me in and treated me like their own son. While staying with Eli, I normally woke up bright and early to do my chores. One of the chores was milking one of the cows. I had milked before, but this was the first time I was responsible for a cow. I also ended up getting jobs with some other Amish carpenters. Eli had a barnyard with farm animals, so it was a good experience for me to learn how to do many things, like hitching up horses and driving wagons. One time, I came home from working with the local carpenters and the veterinarian was just driving away. Eli looked very, very tired. He was raising two Belgian colts, draft horses that could pull heavy machinery. I call them colts because of their age, but they were probably over 1500 pounds. As it turned out, the boar in the barnyard had taken a swipe at the underbelly of one of the colts and left an eight-inch gap that took the artery. Blood was just gushing out. Eli had pinched the artery with his finger to keep the horse alive until the veterinarian could come and stitch him up. Eli's quick thinking and the gentle nature of Belgians, as well as help from a family member running to a neighbor to call the vet, saved a huge investment. This left a lasting impact on me.

It wasn't until the next summer that I made it to Cape Cod. I spent a couple of months working with Andrew. We did very little fishing because his boat was in dry dock getting repaired. When we finally got it ready, fog had settled in and with no sonar, we weren't able to go out and fish. Because Andrew was a resident of Cape Cod, he could go quahogging, which is the native term for raking for clams. I could join him, but I couldn't rake. When we weren't eating fresh codfish, we were eating fresh quahogs on the half shell; you have to be from Cape Cod to appreciate them! Being with them was a fantastic opportunity for fellowship and to heal from the abusive and controlling situation we had all been under.

CHAPTER 9

BRANCHING OUT

I n early 1979, I was in Lobelville, Tennessee, working with a new family to help them build a log house. Titus Martin, an Old Order Mennonite man, was up visiting from Central America, and he invited me to come and visit his community in Belize. They had moved there to get away from the worldliness of the United States. I decided to go on this adventure, so I went to work picking apples in Pennsylvania, and then bicycled to Tennessee to work in a sawmill to make money for the trip. On the way, I stopped and visited Old Order communities.

I eventually hitchhiked to New Orleans and looked for a ship heading to Belize. While there, I met a group called People of the Living God. These missionaries evangelized on the docks and on the ships, giving out Gospel tracks. I eventually found a ship ready to sail to South America. The captain had two crewmembers that had jumped ship, and he offered me a job on the freighter, which was heading to Venezuela. I was tempted but didn't want to do it alone, so I contacted a friend who, unfortunately, wasn't interested at the time. I still hoped I could make my way on tramp freighters and eventually work my way to Belize. Instead, I flew to Belize City and traveled to Barton Creek to visit Titus's community. While living with them, I learned a lot about tropical farming and ranching and how to swing a machete.

I was still intrigued with colonial and pre-colonial history, so whenever I was near historical sites, I toured them. My fascination with the Mayans had persisted, and I was determined to see Tikal. An eighteen-year-old Mayan boy named Nacasio, who had been adopted by an Amish family, was living in the Barton Creek community. He was unusual in this setting: a Mayan kid speaking Pennsylvania Dutch, Belizean Creole, and Mopan and living in an Amish community. He wanted to go and visit his biological parents but was ashamed of his heritage. I wanted to go to southern Belize to the villages and Tikal, so we teamed up. We traveled west into Guatemala, and then traveled south to the bottom side of Belize. It really troubled me that he was ashamed of his heritage. There we were at the Mayan ruins in Tikal, a beautiful site proving the great history and accomplishments of his ancestors, and he was unable to see past the current state of his culture. I spent a lot of time with him, encouraging him not to be proud of the alcoholism and abuse of his parents but to be proud that he come from a great heritage full of mathematicians and astronomers, a mighty civilization. Impossible to ignore, however, was that they did have a very dark side, which included the practice of human sacrifice.

Nacasio didn't speak Spanish but did speak Mopan Mayan, which used the Spanish numerical system, so when it came to buying, he knew a lot of the modern Mayan words that were the same as the Spanish words. My Spanish, fortunately, was somewhat good. Our teamwork benefitted us but confused those with whom we bargained. Folks just didn't know what to do with a Mayan who spoke both Pennsylvania Dutch and Belizean Creole (Pidgin English) and a Caucasian American who spoke some Spanish. As we traveled, it was scary going to Guatemala from Belize. Lucas Garcia, the Guatemalan president, looked just like Hitler. Elections were fraudulent, and most of the poor peasants in his country opposed his oppressive regime. This was in the heat of their civil war, and travel was dangerous.

But my true call to Guatemala came in 1981. Belize was given independence on September 21st of that year, and there was fear that once the British left, the Guatemalan army would roll in and reclaim Belize because of a one-hundred-year-old border dispute. I traveled with a Mennonite guy named John Culp who wanted to visit some of the pastors he knew at Mennonite Air Missions in Guatemala City. Not long before, when I had been staying at the Mennonite Center in Belize City, I had met Pastors Harold Kaufman and Victor and Juan Ovalle. At the time, they had left Guatemala for Belize because they feared for their lives after some death threats. A Mennonite missionary, John Troyer, was killed shortly before this in Palama, Chimaltenango, in front of his wife and children. Dorcas Hoover documented the story in her book called *Awaiting the Dawn* in 1992. The pastors invited me to visit them if I ever got back to Guatemala. John and I took a flight from Tikal/Flores to Guatemala City late in December 1981 and arrived on New Year's Eve. When we got to Mennonite Air Missions, we were exhausted and went to bed, but I remember waking up to all kinds of explosions. Fortunately, it was just fireworks. However, guerrillas had firebombed five nearby gas stations that night. A lot of displaced Christians were staying in the city because of the fighting.

I quickly got to know one of the local deacons, Bartolo, who was from the Quiche Department. He had been given two weeks to decide if he'd join the insurgency. Eighteen days later, they came back after dark, knocked on the door, and told him to come out. They warned him that if he didn't, they'd come in and get him. As he went out the door, he had a vision of Jesus speaking to him telling him it would be all right. He didn't want his wife and daughter to get hurt. They tied him up and shot him with a 22-caliber gun, but the bullet didn't have much impact. So they put a ball and cap gun to his forehead and shot him at point blank range. Instead of lead in the chamber, they had rocks and beans. He later told us how he watched himself as he floated above his body in the air and saw what was happening. He saw a man in white, Jesus, beckoning him to come back into his body. He went back into his body, and his life was restored. The men were afraid and took off running. He remembers Jesus helping him back to the house and vividly remembers Jesus having a towel draped over his arm. He was unconscious for three days, and during that time, friends from the

San Bartolomé Jocotenango church took him to Guatemala City. In a vision, he experienced Jesus taking him to the city. He was flying over the area and saw things that had happened or were going to happen. When he awoke in Guatemala City, before others could tell him what had happened, he was able to describe everything because Jesus had shown him.

Another miracle occurred when a woman and man were dragged off a bus by the army. Typically, they put the people on the side of the cliff and shot them so that their lifeless bodies rolled down the cliff. This man started rolling down the cliff, and as he rolled, they shot at him. His wife was sure he was dead. At the same time, he heard the shooting and thought she had been killed. Instead, they both returned to their home to find each other alive.

This was my second time in Guatemala but my first time in the city. These miracles were amazing. Sometimes it takes a war. As King David spoke in Psalm 91:2, "I will say of the Lord, He is my refuge and my fortress: my God; in him will I trust."

In early 1981, I spent most of my time in southern Belize with the Mayans and a couple of different missionary groups. The first group included independent missionaries, Leonard and Fanny Kropf, and their six children. They were Mennonites and part of a group of missionaries that used the phrase "evangelization through colonization." Fanny came to Belize as a teenager with her parents, Jerry and Katie Troyer, as a part of the same Amish community that Levi Mast and Joe J. Miller were members of in Pilgrimage Valley near San Ignacio. Later, most of the group moved ten miles away to Barton Creek. This was the community that Titus Martin had invited me to. These folks had moved to Belize and adopted the new country as theirs, making a living while setting up a small church in the San Pedro Toledo district. They raised chickens and cattle. Each Thursday and Friday, they'd butcher 150 chickens and take them to market in Punta Gorda in the Toledo district. The Kropfs had joined me that previous summer and fall in Mt. Pleasant Mills, Pennsylvania, for the apple-picking season. Herb Apple Orchard provided housing for workers and paid ten dollars a bin (about 1000 pounds of apples), which was not too bad at that time since we paid no rent or utilities. I could pick up to five bins a day. During their time in the States, Leonard bought an old school bus and lots of supplies to take back to Belize. I had put the Hodaka 125 two-stroke dirt bike I had bought on the bus.

They had expected to be gone for four months, but it turned into six months when Leonard was offered a job in his hometown of Dixon, Illinois, skinning muskrats and raccoons for the trapping season. I visited them after I stopped to see family in Wisconsin, planning to drive down with them. When Leonard extended their stay to make extra money, I told them I would go ahead and take buses through Mexico and meet them in Belize in a month. Leonard had left his house and farm in the care of one of the Mayan families in the church he pastored. I later met up with them in the San Ignacio Cayo district at Jerry and Katie's and drove down with them to the San Pedro, Toledo District. I'll never forget seeing the look on the Mayan family's face when we arrived at the farm. They told us they'd heard Leonard had died in a plane crash!

It was almost four years before when two members of the Lynyrd Skynrd Band, along with their backup singer Cassie Gaines, died in a plane crash and the anniversary of the crash had been mentioned on Radio Belize. Since the only Leonard they knew was Leonard Kropf they were positive it was he. Because, in their minds, Leonard was dead they decided to break open the storage bin that held about a ton of beans and began to eat them. Then they decided that rotating the cattle in different pastures was too much work, so they just let them eat down all the pasture that resulted in eliminating the backup pastures the Kropfs had always maintained. This was in the early part of the dry season, so it was not a good move. I could see the frustration in Leonard's face, but being a forgiving person, he tried not to show it.

On our drive down the Hummingbird Highway, we picked up two hitchhikers. They were biology students from an east coast university that wanted to spend a few days in the bush collecting insects and catching bats. We told them we would try to find them a guide in San Pedro. We went to the mayor and asked him for information on who could guide them. The locals were suspicious of anyone going unguided into the bush because they worried they might find a marijuana plantation. We found a guide and Ronny, Leonard's eleven-year-old son, and I joined them. Our guide had a twenty-gauge single-shot shotgun and a machete, and I had my machete.

On the second day of hiking, one of the guys was about fifty yards behind the rest of us and hollered, "I found a yellow jaw!" We all ran back, hoping he knew enough to stay back. When he pointed to where the snake was hiding, I had to give myself time to focus because it was so well camouflaged. I told him that it wasn't a yellow jaw but a tommy goff (jumping pit viper). When I told him it could jump over half the length of its body, he thought I was lying. He was poking it with a stick and making it mad. Our guide pointed his twenty-gauge shotgun at it, but before he could fire the guy said, "Live and let live."

Since they were paying him, the guide didn't kill it. But over the next two days, he shared enough snake stories that the guys decided if their wife and kids walked barefoot in the jungle daily, they too would kill every poisonous snake they saw. On our return, the guide remembered exactly where it had been and would have killed it had it still been there, but it had moved on.

Later that day, we heard a lot of noise and the guide told us to step up on a tree that was lying over and stay still. A large herd of wild boars walked through, rooting up bugs and roots. I started counting and realized there were about 200 boars in the herd. At one point, we were surrounded and a big boar started sniffing. After smelling us, he started to clack his tusks together as a warning to the rest of the herd. I grasped my machete, thinking I might have to start swinging. Fortunately, they all ran away and our guide told us if he had brought his dog along, they would have probably attacked the dog and us. Years before, the boars would certainly have killed us. They would surround the victim and eventually tear him apart. When the sapodilla trees were found to produce chicle sap, the Wrigley Gum Company hired workers to live on the trail throughout the production season to gather the gap to make their gum. These workers had guns, and the boars learned to be scared of humans because of those guns. In 1961, after Hurricane Hattie's destruction, the workers disappeared, but the boars seemed to have retained their fear.

I had a run-in with a tommy goff snake a year later while walking on a trail from Santa Teresa to Machaca. This was a trail that was not very well traveled, and the villagers in Santa Teresa refused to let me travel it without a guide. One of the men had someone in Machaca that owed him money, so he showed me the way. Even though I showed them I had a compass and the topographic map of the area made by the British army, they still insisted I use a guide. We took turns taking the lead and at one point, when he was in front, he stopped and said he needed a long branch to kill a snake. I just handed him my machete, which was a lot longer than the one he had. He took the backside of the machete, broke the snake's back, picked it up with the machete, and threw it to the side. Had I been in front I probably wouldn't have seen it.

The second group I was involved with was the Caribbean Light and Truth Missions in Southern Belize, another Mennonite missionary group. Originating in eastern Iowa, this mission was funded by a very small association of conservative Mennonite churches led by a man named Wilford Stutzman. Their goal was, and is, to do church planting amidst the Kekchi and Mopan Mayan Indians in Southern Belize. Today, two of Wilford's sons are still missionaries there.

In a leap forward, in 2015 while in Minnesota, I learned about a group of former Hutterites who were worshiping in Canton, Ohio through some of the Hutterites who had been donating and volunteering with Hope Haven International. I went to their church service, and the person I sat next to said, "You're Mark Richard! I'm Gayland, and we worked together with Mennonite Air Missions in Guatemala in the late '80s." He had been a missionary and had been in Guatemala at the same time Sandy and I were there.

After the service, I went up to the guest speaker and introduced myself. He turned out to be Steven Stutzman, Wilford's youngest son, from Belize. At this service there were only two non-Hutterites besides me, and I had a connection with both of them. I'm constantly amazed at the beautiful tapestry the Lord weaves as people come in and out of my life. "As every man hath received the gift, even so minister the same one to another, as good stewards of the manifold grace of God." (1 Peter 4:10)

In April 1982, there was a wedding at the Red Creek Beachy Amish church where Fanny Kropf's family attended, near San Ignacio in Belize. While I was there, I met some folks who had come to the wedding from central Honduras and they invited me to visit their Beachy Amish community in Guaimaca. I decided to take one of the dugout canoes that banana workers used for transportation to come and go from the Honduras. It was sixty miles across the shipping channel from Mango Creek, Belize, to Puerto Cortes, Honduras, and it was the fastest route. Belize had a banana industry and a lot of workers came from Honduras, hired because they would work more cheaply than the locals. A couple of times a week, these canoes, each with a forty-horse outboard motor, would shuttle workers back and forth for the equivalent of about five dollars. I took the regularly scheduled trip, which was always at night. I met a young man on the boat who was from Tulsa, Oklahoma. He had just finished his stint with the Peace Corp and wanted to see Honduras. These canoes rode very low in the water, and the seas were typically calmer at night. It took most of the night, around seven or eight hours, to get across. The homemade life-vests were waterlogged and useless. That night, it wasn't too bad until four hours into the trip when the sea waves grew high. The water splashed on the carburetor, causing the motor to die. We started bobbing around the sea like a cork. There was lots of praying in that little boat until the captain got the motor going again. This ride was definitely not for the faint at heart!

When in Honduras, we had our passports stamped by an extremely young soldier who was trying to read them upside down. He was obviously illiterate. We then took buses up to Tegucigalpa, the capital. After finding a hotel, we went to get something to eat, and as we walked down the street, two undercover police officers asked us for our passports. One of them had flashed his badge so quickly that I started to get suspicious, thinking that he wasn't really a policeman but someone who wanted to steal our passports. I grabbed it away with a fast swipe, but when he didn't back down and showed his badge again, I realized that I had made a big mistake. My friend had left his passport in the hotel room. They eventually let us continue, but the police checked on us again in the morning. There was a civil war going on at that time and the police were suspicious of anyone new to the town, probably for good reason.

The next day, we split ways, and I traveled about fifty miles to Guaimaca and the Mennonite community where the folks lived whom I had met at the wedding. This community had originally been established as an Old Order Amish horse-and-buggy community with no modern conveniences. They had left the Old Order and joined the Beachy Amish/Mennonite who used tractors and cars. I spent a few days with them. From there, I traveled across to southwest Honduras and up the length of El Salvador to visit other Mennonite communities. This was the worst time to travel through El Salvador and not very smart on my part. El Salvador was in the midst of a twelve-year civil war, which had begun in 1980. One of the more famous events publicized around the world during this time was the brutal murder of four missionary nuns. The missionaries and church-workers in this country were no safer than the citizens.

Next, I spent some time at an orphanage just east of San Salvador. I then stayed a few days with another Mennonite family, the Glicks, who lived as part of the local community, similar to the Kropfs. The Glicks had a small clinic because Eli's wife was a nurse. Eli had laying hens and sold eggs to support their work. Just after I visited them, Eli's son and eight others were in their small pickup truck, coming back from a church meeting at night when the American volunteer driver didn't stop at a roadblock. The soldiers started firing on them, thinking they were part of the insurgency. When they finally stopped, there were many bullet holes in the pickup and Eli's son had gotten a small graze on his neck. With that many bullets and that many people in the truck, it was a miracle no one was killed. When the truck got back to the Glicks and Eli saw all of the holes, he praised the Lord because he knew angels had protected them.

When I left Eli Glick's place, I was able to get a ride to the entrance of the next town with a customer who was there to buy eggs. While I waited for the bus, a woman with a three-year-old little girl walked up and begged me to take her daughter to the United States. She was living in fear and dire poverty and desperately wanted the best for her child. Many kids were starving and dying at that time. Of course, I couldn't take her, but it left a lasting impression of the horrible effects of hunger and fear on these impoverished people in war-torn El Salvador. Eventually, the bus came and I was able to get on. We were only a few miles from the army checkpoint where we were pulled over. When they found out where I had boarded the bus, they believed my story was fishy since I had gotten on in the middle of nowhere. They took me at gunpoint to their officer and the bus left. When I explained to him what I had been doing, thankfully the story made sense, as he was familiar with the Glicks. After searching my backpack and finding my Bible, he told the soldiers I was a pastor and from that point on they were very nice. They stopped the next vehicle that went by and asked them to give me a ride to the Guatemalan border, only a few miles away. I said goodbye and thanked the Lord for His protective care!

I headed to Mennonite Air Missions in Guatemala City. I was going to the Wycliffe headquarters because Caribbean Light and Truth had asked me to pick up the new translation of the Kekchi Bible, a major Mayan dialect. They already had the New Testament translation, but this was the first complete Bible in Kekchi. I went to the Wycliffe headquarters and paid for a case of Bibles, which they didn't have on-site. They sent me about five hours away to Coban, Alta Verapaz, where many Kekchi speakers lived. I picked up the Bibles at the home of Francis and Ruth, the Wycliffe Bible translators. (Fast forward to over thirty-five years later, while in Coban during a Rotary funded wheelchair-seating clinic, I went to visit my old friend Verton Miller from Belize. Verton and his family had bought the house from Ruth and Francis and were involved with the delivery of the Kekchi Bibles.) I then took the bus back to Puerto Barrios and rode a ferry to a village called Livingston in order to take a boat to Punta Gorda, Belize. Unfortunately, I found out that because of the "saber rattling" between Belize and Guatemala, the border had been shut down. They had closed down the ferry service between Livingston, Guatemala, and Punta Gorda, Belize, so I tried to hire a dugout canoe operator, which was illegal for the Belizeans. I had a rendezvous scheduled on the beach with him, but he got scared and didn't pick me up.

So, I traveled back towards Guatemala City for an hour and took the highway north towards the Peten Department and started hiking the jungle trail above the Rio Dulce River, called the Quebrada Seca. At that point I had about seventy pounds of Kekchi Bibles and a fifty-pound backpack. Arriving after dark, I strung my hammock between two trees just one hundred yards up the trail. I was sleeping when, early in the morning, I felt someone staring at me. It was a curious Mayan man. I knew how to ask directions in both Mopan and Kekchi, the local Mayan languages, so I managed to get him to help me to the next village. I paid him a couple of bucks to carry the Bibles, and as I continued on, I found others who were willing to carry them for pay.

After a full day of hiking, I got to a village called Dolores on the Belizean side of the border. I still had thirteen miles to go and was exhausted. In Dolores, I found a family that let me stay in their hut. They agreed to carry the case of Bibles to Crique Sarco later that day, as they knew the Mennonite missionaries. They also told me that the local Catholic priest was in Dolores for a mass. The priest was from the Garifuna people, but served the Mayan as well as the Garifuna. He was excited about the Bibles and wanted them all. I shared a few with him, and the next day I walked the thirteen miles to Crique Sarco and stayed with some Mennonite missionaries, glad to be back in Belize. The Bibles arrived a few hours after I did. The following day, I took their boat up the Temash River to Punta Gorda. I then traveled back inland to where Caribbean Light and Truth was headquartered at Blue Creek. Throughout the two-and-a-half week journey I nearly drowned, was detained by police, and became lost in the jungle, but I was saved from it all, and I got the Bibles!

A lot of the missionaries had their families with them in Belize and couldn't, or wouldn't, have taken the trip to get the Bibles because of the danger. Once back in Punta Gorda, I had to go to Belize immigration and explain the journey to them. Even though it wasn't the accepted way to enter Belize, they thought it was fine. Belize was relatively safe at that point. The British army was doing their jungle training there and had a stabilizing presence. Had they not been there, Guatemala might have invaded and taken over Belize.

A few months later, while I was in Crique Sarco, two of the nurses that were working there asked if I'd meet with the British major about his promise to build a wooden bridge across the Temash River. At that time, you had to swim or take a dugout canoe to get across it. It was no more than one hundred feet across, but it still made it difficult for the nurses to do their work. The British Army was planning on using the Napali Gurkhas to do this building. The Gurkhas were tribal people who were fierce warriors—the only group the British Army couldn't defeat. Instead, they allowed them to become British soldiers. At the meeting, the British major agreed to build the bridge as long as the locals readied the logs. Unfortunately, a week later the Argentinians invaded the Falkland Islands, and all of the Gurkhas packed up and headed there to fight. This was in late April 1982. The bridge was never completed.

During this time, I would take my turn delivering school books from the school library to a boy by the name of Sebastian who lived about eight miles away. Sebastian probably had undiagnosed muscular dystrophy. He was around nine years old, and a few years before, he had started to lose his muscle tone. At this time, he lived his life in a hammock. His family would take him and his hammock outside during the day and then bring him back in for the night. They lived in a new town called Jordan Village. Jordan Village didn't have a school, but Sebastian had been able to learn to read in the village where he had been brought up. He took the books we brought him every week and read to the children in the village. I wanted to get him a wheelchair, but before I could, Sebastian died. This haunted me for the next five years.

In 1983, one of the pastor's sons, Nicholas, found a cave with petroglyphs in it while hunting. I had read a National Geographic article about a similar find just a few years before in Guatemala, not more than fifteen miles away and remembered the government had sent a team of archaeologists from National Geographic down immediately. I knew this was a big find and asked Nicholas if he would take me with him to see it. Pastor Macario wouldn't let his son go until his work was done, so I ended up helping him burn about five acres of jungle that had been cut a few months before so they could plant. The next day, Nicholas took me to where they had hunted for gibnut, a nocturnal rodent, which the dogs had chased into a cave. The Mayans were too superstitious to go into a cave because they believed caves were entrances to the underworld. Because Nicholas was a Christian, he was not afraid to go in and found the pots and drawings on the wall. This was more like graffiti than the previous Naj Tunich cave find in Guatemala, but it was within the Mayan Classic period, which was considered the golden age of Mayan history. I took pictures, had them developed, and gave them to a Wycliffe linguist who knew the minister of archaeology and Premier George Price. This was on the Belize side of the border, less than twenty-five miles from Aguateca. National Geographic came down to assess this find within a few weeks of my report.

In the jungle, you shouldn't sleep on the ground so I had designed my own mosquito-proof tent fly for a hammock. I had been asked by two of the local nurses to go and check out a new jungle village, which had popped up on the Belize side of the border. Due to the Guatemalan civil war, Belize was getting some of their refugees because it was considered safer. Belize had an area called a reserve where the Mayans could live, surviving by hunting and "slash and burn" farming. They lived within the reserve but couldn't own the land, similar in some ways to an American Indian reservation. The nurses were wondering if the children were getting vaccinations and what level of health care was available in the community. At this time, I had the little two-stroke, 125cc Hodaka motorcycle, so I used it to travel as far as I could toward the village of Jalacte. Because of the rough trail, I parked the motorcycle about a day's hike away, under the thatch overhang of a Kekchi hut, and hiked up the jungle trail to the village. I arrived, only to find that the men of the village had taken their crop of beans to market to sell. To do this, each man probably carried about one hundred pounds of beans on his back. By tradition, you were supposed to communicate with only the men when you entered a village, so I walked across the river to camp for the night, planning to come back in the morning when the men were back. I did, however, glean enough information from the women to learn they were still getting health care from the Guatemalan side. This is really what the nurses needed to know.

The next morning, I woke up and noticed a bunch of ants under my backpack. When I moved the backpack, there was a yellow-jaw or "fer-de-lance," an extremely poisonous snake, under it. A well-known rule of the jungle is that you don't cut a yellow-jaw in half with a machete because the other end could still come after you. Instead, you break it's back. Another recommendation—rule—is to hit the back of the snake's neck using the backside of the machete. I had my machete stuck in the ground holding mosquito netting away from the gas stove while making oatmeal for breakfast. Fortunately, this was a small snake, so I did end up cutting it with my machete, efficiently slicing it into six pieces because it was coiled up. Life in the jungle is always dangerous.

In the fall of 1983, I stayed with the Kendricks in Cut and Shoot, Texas. Jeff was a contractor at the time. Eventually, Jeff and his wife Jeana would go on to direct Door of Hope International's (DOHI) literature distribution into Eastern Europe and DOHI's Texas office. They would spend half of the year at the Door of Hope based in Austria, near the Yugoslavian border. They and their teams smuggled thousands of Bibles into Yugoslavia, Hungary, Romania, Bulgaria, Poland, CSSR (Czechoslovakia), and the Soviet Union during the Cold War.

Years before, in 1972 and 1973, Jeff and Jeana had attended the same church in Pueblo, Colorado as my brother, Denny. Before they were saved, the two had become involved with drugs and sold them for a living. A decade later, God took the very worst of their lives and turned it into something beautiful. Their experiences as drug dealers turned out to be a big help when they became believers, especially for smuggling Bibles. When Jeff first came to know Jesus, he wanted to be a carpenter like Him. By His grace, Jeff became a successful contractor.

In the early '80s, both Jeff and Jeana felt a calling to minister personally in Communist lands but didn't think they could ever afford to do it. They had been supporting missions that ministered there for about eight years. At the time, *New Life Magazine* asked Jeff to write an article about such organizations. Jeff and his wife traveled to Los Angeles and interviewed several of the largest ministries working in Communist countries. When they interviewed Paul Popov, the president of DOHI, he asked them to fill out applications because their base in Austria needed extensive remodeling. Jeff told him they couldn't afford to go, but Paul insisted they fill out the forms. A few months later, he phoned and asked them to consider going if God provided.

Miraculously, Jeff made enough extra money to go. Paul told them that when he had looked over their applications, he had a special feeling about them. They worked in Eastern Europe for thirteen years, smuggling Bibles overseas half of the year and interviewing and training Bible couriers stateside for the other half of the year. Jeff and Jeana still work with DOHI from their home in Texas.

DOHI, originally Evangelism to Communist Lands, was founded by Paul's father, Haralan Popov, who spent thirteen and a half years in Communist prisons for his faith in Christ. At the time of his arrest, he was pastoring the largest evangelical church in Bulgaria. His story can be found in his book, *Tortured for His Faith*.

I worked for Jeff for a few months in late 1984 as a carpenter. Jeff was hoping I would decide not to return to Guatemala and join them for the summer of 1985 to help smuggle Bibles. This was a real temptation but I was convinced that my calling was in Guatemala.

CHAPTER 10

NURTURING EACH OTHER

lthough I didn't see Kenny a lot during my turbulent years, we had remained close. Like me, he loved travel and history and was gifted at making friends. Kenny, similar to all of my brothers, was the kind of person who would give you the shirt off his back. He loved to cook and prepared meals, always happy to invite homeless people in to eat. This turned into a Thanksgiving tradition. Kenny was a lot like my parents: very generous, enjoyed helping people, and never really saved a lot of money because he always gave it away.

In 1984, Kenny drove his little Datsun pickup down to Georgia where I was working, planting trees. This was a crew made up of the families I had known from Horseshoe, Florida—fishermen. Because fishing was seasonal, this was a way to make decent money if you worked hard. Some of the crew could plant over 10,000 seedlings in a day. If tree planting were an Olympic sport, my friend Jeff Reed would have had the gold medal. Years later, Jeff's father learned how to pull temporary work visas for Mayans from the HueHuetenango Department of Guatemala.

Planting pine trees was a mixed blessing. It was a seasonal job, but it allowed us to camp with no expenses, except for food, as we lived in campers that were converted school buses. I was the only one in the crew who camped outside. I had made a tent fly for my parachute hammock that I slept in for about two months while we planted the seedlings. It was sad to see that they had clear-cut the hardwoods while logging, just to make room to plant pine, which was used for the paper industry. They did use the hickory for railroad cross ties but lots of good wood was left to burn. At that time, hickory was used mainly for baseball bats and firewood. Today, it is used for flooring and cabinets. It was the hardest physical job I have ever done.

With help from my friends at the church in Horseshoe Beach, Florida, I made enough money to return to volunteering in Belize and Guatemala. Kenny and I drove to Brownsville, Texas, put Kenny's pickup in storage, and took public transportation through Mexico. Kenny wanted to volunteer with me, but first, we stopped at Palenque, one of the Mayan sites in Chiapas, Mexico and spent a couple of days touring and visiting. All of our possessions were in our backpacks, and we slept where we could find a place to hang our hammocks. We traveled over to the Yucatan Peninsula and visited Tulum, another beautiful archaeological site overlooking the Caribbean. Enjoying our passion for the Mayan ruins, we went on to visit Altun Ha, Xunantunich, Nim Li Punit, and Lubaantun in Belize, as well as Tikal, Uaxactun, and Quirigua in Guatemala. Last, we visited Copan in Honduras. When we were in Belize we also visited our Mennonite friends.

When Kenny and I were down in the Toledo district of Belize trekking over the jungle mountain pass, we met a couple of Kekchi Mayans who thought we were archaeologists. We came upon them on the Sa Blanc River where they were fishing. They caught fish by using crunched leaves to poison the fish that swam in small pools in the river, as it was the dry season. They had been trying to loot an archaeological site with no luck. The aspiring looters were frustrated because they couldn't find any gold. The steles, slabs that had the Mayan hieroglyphs carved into them, had fallen over and were on their sides. They thought if they could read them that maybe they could find the gold. We convinced them our friend could interpret the glyphs on the steles for them. Jeff McKennon was a high school teacher from Lafollette High School in Madison, Wisconsin, the high school we attended in the fall of 1968. He was now a professor at the University of Wisconsin and a Mayan researcher. I convinced them that if they took us to the site, we'd photograph the hieroglyphs and find out what they said. This site in Belize turned out to be the largest populated Mayan city ever found in southern Belize. I got the pictures developed the following week in Guatemala City and took them to the Wycliffe headquarters in Guatemala City. Matthew and Rose Mary Urick were the linguists who translated the New Testament into Mopa Mayan, the dialect spoken in this area of Belize. Matthew named the site Uxbenka meaning Old Place in Mopan. He then sent copies to the Ministry of Archaeology in Belmopan, Belize. Ironically, one of the potential looters, Juan, ended up being hired by the Ministry of Archaeology as the caretaker for the site.

Kenny and I took buses up to the Mexican border. We found ourselves on a chicken bus half full of Honduranians wanting to get into the States illegally. Back then, they were fleeing from the civil wars in Central America. Today, they're fleeing from the gang violence. This was during the time when the government had instituted the civil patrols. The Guatemalan Army used some of the same strategies used in Vietnam, such as strategic hamlets (the army would come in and would tell them they had to stay in a defined area or they would be killed) and the civil patrols. The army figured if they scripted the men into the patrol, there was less chance they would join the guerrillas.

On the bus ride from Quetzaltenango to the Mexican border at La Mesilla, less than a hundred miles, we were stopped ten times by the patrol. About half the time, everyone had to get off the bus and show his or her identification. Sometimes, they let the women and children stay on. Some of the patrols had guns, but other times they just had sticks. At one of the checkpoints, the patrol wanted to confiscate Kenny's pocketknife. Kenny, being very attached to his pocketknife, stood his ground and said they had no right to it. It was a little dicey for a bit. They finally backed down and Kenny got to keep his five-dollar knife and we got to keep our lives.

Throughout 1983 and 1984, weavers often approached me wanting me to buy their crafts. I was living on a very tight budget and couldn't afford to purchase their products. I found myself feeling very uncomfortable with the concept of making money by buying and selling crafts that the local people were making, often observing them being taken advantage of. I saw a lot of abuse, like when the poor widow who, when desperate to sell, sold her crafts for less than half of what the product was worth. I saw it in action among the native people themselves, who encouraged me to buy and sell while making money by taking advantage of the poor. There was no tourism in Guatemala at that time except for a few backpackers and competition was fierce in the local markets. I had a choice and decided I could help these poor families. I quickly learned that we could buy high-quality, hand-woven, wool blankets and find a good market for them in the States. In 1983, I brought two blankets back and sold them quickly.

I determined I could hire one of the local pastors to do the purchasing for me. This would financially help the pastor, and even with a small mark-up for my costs, the weavers would still make very good money. The next year, I went back with Francisco, the local Guatemalan pastor's father, and traveled to the Department of Totonicapan. This was an area that contained one of the highest Mayan populations in the country, with around ninety-eight percent of the citizens being pure Mayan. We started with the town of Momostenango, wanting to purchase blankets. In the markets, we found we were always dealing with a middleman. So, we started walking through hillsides, looking for local weavers. We soon found Emilio Axup and his family, which included a daughter, Clara Luz, who had spina bifida.

Emilio and his family's cottage industry was weaving and selling wool blankets. Each member of the family was involved. Emilio weaved, his wife carded the wool, his mother spun the wool, his son took the blankets to the hot springs to wash and shrink them out, and his other daughter brushed them to pull out the nap. When we found them, they took the blankets to the market and hoped they could sell them to a middleman or someone from Guatemala City. The market was competitive and the country was in the heat of the civil war, making it dangerous to travel. We set up a schedule. Every two weeks, Francisco would go to Emilio and five other families in the area and buy weavings. I made a simple catalog of pictures of blankets and let them know what people liked.

We mailed the blankets back to Madison, Wisconsin, where several of my friends sold them. When I was in the States, I would take blankets to craft shows. After Sandy and I were married in 1985, we did the powwow circuit in the upper Midwest, selling blankets at the events. I would call Francisco's son and put in an order every other week, telling him what to buy. We used a joint checking account to get money to the families quickly.

For the next three years, we continued to help, guiding the weavers with quality control feedback. For instance, they didn't understand that the Americans wanted natural dyes. Instead, they assumed that the North Americans and Europeans would want chemical dyes, which produced brighter primary colors. I encouraged them to go back to the natural colors produced by using products from nature.

After being in Guatemala for the first five months of 1985, I flew back to Miami, Florida and took a bus to Horseshoe Beach where Sandy's brother Keith, his family, and their mother Jean were staying. While visiting Sandy's mother, she reneged on her warning about "staying away from those Richard boys" and encouraged me to get ahold of Sandy. She was worried about her because Sandy was still in The Assembly. She hoped that by playing matchmaker, I might have some influence on her. I gave her my brother's phone number in Cross Plains, Wisconsin, where I would be working that summer.

A week later, Sandy called me from Idaho. She was disillusioned after being in the group for over twelve years, the victim of much spiritual abuse. By this time, Keith had come up to Wisconsin and was also anxious for her to break free of the group. I offered to send her money via Western Union for a plane ticket to come home.

We had so much in common but had not been in contact for seven years. After a short courtship, we married at the end of the summer. The ceremony was held near her family in Bradenton, Florida because most of our friends and family were scattered all over. After the wedding, we moved back to Madison, Wisconsin. I was still doing the community development work with the weavers, so we spent that fall traveling to craft shows and powwows. By mid-December, we loaded up the VW van, visited family in California, and drove to Guatemala through the Baja.

We drove through Mexico City, which is a challenge in the best of circumstances, but at that time they were still cleaning up from the September 19th earthquake, three and a half months before, and it was even more difficult. In addition, we needed to find a VW dealership for some parts for the van. Harold Kaufman, the founder of Mennonite Air Missions, was on furlough so we stayed at his house, just two blocks from the Mission headquarters in Zone 7 of Guatemala City. We continued our volunteer work and worked with the weavers. After three months, we drove back to Wisconsin. I resigned myself to the belief that I was never going back to Guatemala.

By the fall of 1986, Sandy was expecting our first son, Michael, and we moved from Wisconsin to Florida. She wanted to be near her mom, Jean, who still lived in Bradenton. During her years in the Assembly, Jean had delivered all of the babies. Since she was a midwife and we wanted Michael born at home, we felt like we needed to move. Michael was born on the first day of spring in 1986.

Michael's birth was a home birth, and it was a very hard labor for Sandy. Michael was so big that he became stuck in the birth canal. Sandy was losing her strength, so I called Jeana Kendrick, who in addition to working for DOHI was also a midwife back in Texas, for advice. She encouraged us to go to the hospital, so we called an ambulance and went to Manatee County Hospital. They wouldn't let me in the delivery room, so I waited in the hall. I have often wondered if Michael would have been born with cerebral palsy had we not made it to the hospital in time.

After Michael was born, we started to think about our next call, as we always considered our move to Florida a temporary one. We wondered if we needed to stay there or if the Lord had other plans for us. It was tempting to stay. We had a good church with a solid home group. I had a good job with a window and door company doing installations and custom work. My boss, Bob Mullet, was a great guy to work for and was someone that challenged me spiritually. He had been raised Old Order Amish in Ohio so we had a lot in common.

Back in 1982, while busy with the community development project in Momostenango, I had helped a man named Melvin Kipfer on my trips to and from Guatemala. Melvin had been in charge of the construction projects for the Mennonite Air Missions. He built houses and churches. He had told me about a project where a friend had raised broilers to a certain weight and then sold the chickens, making a pretty good profit while providing work for the church members. He had a real concern for the youth from the Mennonite church in Guatemala because of the civil war. I had known him for four or five years, and he had always talked about wanting to start a farm. One day, I came home from work to discover Sandy had received a letter from Guatemala. Just prior to going to the mailbox she had prayed for direction—asking Him to put His will right in front of her face—so when she opened the letter asking us to come and help, she knew it was God answering her prayer. So my wife agreed to go back with me to Guatemala.

When I told my boss, Bob, that we were called to move to Guatemala to build and direct the boys' farm, I thought he would rejoice. Instead, he expressed concern about whom he could find to take my place in running Mullet's Windows and Doors. This was a spinoff of Mullets Aluminum, his brother Butch's company. I had done most of the installations of sliding glass doors and fixed glass mirror, tub, and shower enclosures, as well as delivered all of the windows for the carpenters to install. They offered me a fifty percent pay increase and my own shop. It was flattering to know how important I was to the company, but I needed to be faithful to the call.

I was told we would be well taken care of by Melvin, the Mennonite man from Canada who was funding the project, so when our church, Ashton Mennonite, offered to support us, I told them we were covered. Unfortunately, little did we know that Melvin's ideal of supporting us was just $200 per month. It was a good thing we had the house we had built to live in and land to grow vegetables, as well as lots of cracked eggs to eat. We didn't feel sorry for ourselves but looked for opportunities to give eggs and vegetables to other under-supported missionaries.

In 1987, Sandy and I made a commitment of two years to help build the farm that would contain 5,000 laying hens in Guatemala. Melvin's desire was to provide a Christian environment for teenage boys who were living in at-risk areas. Because of the civil war, there was a good chance these boys could be dragged off at gunpoint to become part of the war or even killed by the death squads, so this farm was developed as a safe haven for them, while keeping them in a Christian environment. We took in as many as we could and provided them with work and an opportunity to study. In addition to the hens, they grew fruits and vegetables, which we sold to help support the project. The ranch was located twenty-five miles outside Guatemala City at an elevation of 6000 feet. The climate's temperatures seldom reached eighty degrees and rarely fell below fifty, but it usually hit seventy degrees every day. The soil was very fertile, and the climate provided a year-round growing season. They were able to grow crops like avocados, potatoes, cabbage, cauliflower, tomatoes, and corn, which grew up to eighteen feet tall!

In the summer of 1988, the house we were living in was nearing completion. The day we were awaiting had arrived, and electricity was hooked up. The next step would be putting in a well and holding tank for running water. We had built a 220-foot chicken coop and every few months we finished another fifty-foot section. By the time the chicken enclosure was completed, we ended up housing 5000 laying hens. The last section, initially planned for more hens, ended up being used for a dairy cow and some rabbits. It was self-sustaining because it was Melvin's personal project, not part of the Mennonite Mission. Sometimes we felt like the Mission didn't know what to do with Sandy and I because we didn't follow their traditions.

Guatemala was a volatile country. A civil war was raging that lasted from 1960 to 1996. During the 1980s, the Guatemalan military had assumed almost absolute government power for five years. As well as fighting between government forces and rebel groups, the conflict involved a large-scale campaign of one-sided violence by the Guatemalan state against the civilian population. Guatemala was accredited with being the first country in Latin America to engage in the widespread use of forced people disappearances. Thousands of civilians were killed or "disappeared" during the conflict, most at the hands of the military, police, and intelligence services. It was a dangerous time in Guatemala.

PHOTO COLLECTION I

Michael (age 2.5) playing with the children in Sumpango.

*Sabastian from southern Belize spent the last few years of his life in a
hammock after he lost his ability to walk because of Muscular Dystrophy.*

*Dodger Stadium August 1997, Ramon Martinez was
rehabbing from shoulder surgery. He funded the shipping of
200 wheelchairs from Miami to the Dominican Republic.*

Petro Glyph cave in Toledo district of Belize, 1983. The National Geographic showed up shortly after giving copies of this picture to the Mopan Mayan Linguist.

In New York with Diane Sawyer filming a Primetime piece on the Jim Roberts group with Philip and Francesca Haney and Stan Avery.

Joint wheelchair delivery with Samaritan's Purse at a center for children with cerebral palsy in Monrovia, Liberia.

This is a jumping viper (tommygoff) like the ones I ran into in the Belizean bush.

In Gaza in 1999 these soldiers were on guard duty in front of Yasser Arafat's house and they let Sandy pose with them. Moments later, their commanding officer scolded them for letting us take the picture.

Just before the US invasion of Afghanistan, the Mobility Project delivered a few containers of refurbished wheelchairs and PETs to Afghanistan. This girl was brought in a wheelbarrow.

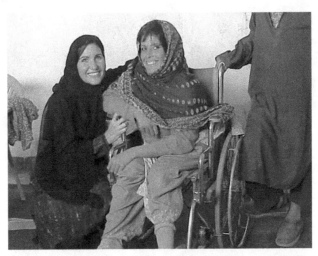

The Mobility Project had to insist to the Taliban leaders that they needed to bring women and children, not just men, to receive wheelchairs.

In 1993 we presented Magda de Serrano, the First Lady of Guatemala, two of Joni's books just before her and her husband were exiled to Panama.

In 1996, on my first trip to Vietnam we found that there were more people needing wheelchairs because of polio than because of the war. Dr. Mike Francis had polio as a child and lost a year of his childhood.

I was with Ken Behring and helped him give away his first wheelchair in Hai Phuong, Vietnam. Ken then founded the Wheelchair Foundation and in about 12 years gave away his millionth wheelchair.

Children that were turned away at the San Juan de Dios Center in Lima, Peru, because there weren't enough wheelchairs.

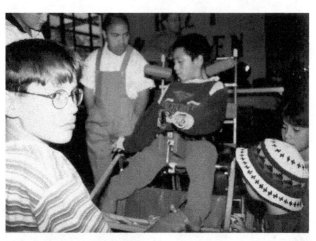

Michael, with Fidel, showing him that even though he couldn't use his hands to write he could use his feet, thanks to the creativity of Richard Stepan who mounted the tray at his feet. Today Fidel drives his power wheelchair using his feet all over town and pulls a Beeline trailer picking up recyclables.

Visiting a Hindu temple in Katmandu, Nepal, were Al McNeese and Mark Hawkins from Western Rehab, Wayne Hanson from ROC Wheels, and a volunteer from Airline Ambassadors.

We were at a wheelchair delivery in Santo Domingo, Ecuador, with the tsachilas.

A meeting in Gaza with Mrs. Intisar Al Wasir, the Minister of Social Affairs, during a wheelchair delivery in January of 2001.

David working with a volunteer to properly seat a young girl in Joyabaj, Quiche Guatemala.

CHAPTER 11

FRUITFULNESS

The Lord continued to work in our lives in unexpected ways. Back in Indiana, we were a part of Reunion 88. Sandy and I had been on a committee that brought over one hundred former Assembly members and their children together. This was a time of healing and served as closure for many of us.

After the reunion, we were delayed in returning to Guatemala. Our truck's motor had to be re-built and the mechanic had run into difficulty. Our delay resulted in an opportunity to lead Lora, Sandy's sister, to Christ. Sandy and I praised the Lord, as we were able to witness the power of God in Lora's life. We watched and prayed as the Lord granted her repentance and mightily touched her life. During those days with us, she often broke out into tears thanking the Lord for her new spiritual eyesight.

At that time, we felt a burden for collecting some used wheelchairs to take to Guatemala for the needy. Before returning to the States, while building the boys ranch, we saw an incident that changed our lives. One day, while driving from Guatemala City to the ranch on the Pan American Highway in San Lucas, Sacatepequez, I saw a woman crawling across the road. Her situation troubled me deeply, and I could not forget this heartbreaking scene. Not too long after, I saw her again, crawling across a congested, four-lane highway. The second time, we were driving at night in the rain. At first glance, I thought I was seeing a dog. She was protected only by a flimsy piece of plastic covering her. She had cut open a truck tire inner tube and wrapped it around her torso for protection as she drug herself over the asphalt. At that point, we decided we would somehow get that woman a wheelchair.

Before the reunion, we had asked a friend of ours, Carl, who used a wheelchair, to help us find used, donated wheelchairs to bring to Guatemala. After the reunion, we returned to Madison, Wisconsin and received a call from Carl to say that he had sixteen wheelchairs ready for us. Carl had put an advertisement in The National Spinal Cord Injury Association's monthly newsletter magazine, which went out to all their members in south central Wisconsin, most of whom had a physically disability. Keith, Sandy's older brother, had also found one chair at a second-hand store. By the end of our stay, we had collected twenty-five wheelchairs. Because we didn't have room for all of them, we sent five of them to Nicaragua through an organization called Wisconsin-Nicaragua Partners, run locally by a Christian friend of Carl's and ours.

When we received word that the Mission's truck and the trailer was ready to be picked up in Lancaster, Pennsylvania, Keith let his oldest son, Dan, take a driveaway car to Washington, D.C. and onto Lancaster. In this way, Dan could accompany me when I drove the rig back to Wisconsin. We picked up the truck and trailer but noticed the used Perkins diesel motor that had been put in the truck to replace the gas one had very low oil pressure. Louis Horst, who had donated the motor, followed us for a while in hopes the oil pressure would go up. An hour and a half later, when we were in Snyder County, we pulled over and realized the motor wouldn't make it to Guatemala. The person who sold Louis the motor had told him it was in good working order. He thought we should return to Lancaster County. I told him that we were just a few miles from an Amish family I had lived with ten years before, so we went to Eli Miller's farm and asked if we could leave the trailer there until we got the motor rebuilt. Eli was the farmer who saved the Belgian colt when I lived with them. Eli suggested we visit an Old Order Mennonite neighbor of his who was a diesel mechanic, so instead of driving back to Lancaster county with both the Mission truck and Louis's truck, we left the truck at Eli's to get it fixed and Louis drove Dan and me to an on-ramp on the Pennsylvania turnpike in Harrisburg. He really wanted us to go to the bus station, but we didn't have enough money for a bus, so we had to hitchhike. Within an hour, we had a direct ride to Rockford, Illinois, which was 750 miles away. I was able to help drive so the guy who picked us up was delighted to get home a half-day earlier than he would have. Within minutes after he dropped us off, we found a ride to where we were staying with Dan's family in Cottage Grove, Wisconsin.

My brother Ken took us in a pickup with a motorcycle trailer that Chad loaned him to Port Trevorton, Pennsylvania to pick up our truck and trailer at Eli's farm. We were able to stop in Nashville and visit Bruce and Nikki Carroll for a few hours, as well as some Amish friends in Lobelville, Tennessee. In Arkansas, the clutch cable burned up on the truck due to an exhaust leak. We drove the 400 miles to Cut N Shoot, Texas, with no clutch! Years before, Chuck Wimberly taught me how to shift without a clutch in the VW we had in the Assembly. By the feel and sound of the motor, I learned to shift at the right time without using the clutch. We stayed on the interstate to avoid stoplights even though it was a bit further. At one point, we had to pull into a weigh station in Texas. We were forced to come to a stop because we were given a red light, meaning we had to be weighed. Thankfully, just before coming to a stop, we were given a green light so we continued on. I was so relieved not to have to explain the problem to the officials. I probably would have had to get a wrecker to get us going because we were on an uphill grade, and the starter would have never allowed us to get going again. We stayed with our friends from DOHI, the Burnichs and the Kendricks, while getting it fixed, which delayed us another week and a half. It was a blessing in disguise because Judy Roberts, the teenage daughter of Becky Sherrill, agreed to come to Guatemala and help Sandy until Matt was born. Judy needed to get her passport and it took a week.

The next five hundred miles went quite smoothly, but then we started to have one flat tire after another. This was in Mexico where the roads were extremely rough, and we were pulling a trailer that weighed ten tons. We had brake troubles three different times, and then one of the trailer axles broke twenty-five miles from the Guatemalan border. Fortunately, we had an extra axle so I was able to replace the broken one. Louis, knowing we were overweight, had thrown on an extra one.

Throughout this, Sandy was dealing with Michael who was sick with pinkeye. We stopped at a local pharmacy, expecting to be given some medication. Instead the pharmacist gave us chamomile tea and said to make the tea and pour it in his eye. He also told us to pour warm milk in his eyes. We were disappointed because we expected medicine. However, to our surprise it worked—the tea cleared the pinkeye right up! I expected to see the use of alternative medicines when I was living with the Amish but not a drug store. To this day, I wish we (the United States) had a healthier blend of prescriptions and more natural treatments. It seems like it would be better if all medical professionals would use everything available and only use drugs when necessary. This pharmacist seemed to understand that there are often alternatives to expensive drugs. On top of this, Sandy was in her seventh month of pregnancy. With our truck barely able to move, we crawled into Guatemala.

In reaching the border, the blessings began. Two missionary brothers were waiting to greet and help us. Driving into Guatemala City that night proved to be another blessing. The view to our left was an active volcano spitting out balls of fire and lava.

"What a fearful yet glorious sight!" I exclaimed.

Soon after returning to our Guatemalan home, we were able to hand out seven wheelchairs. I searched for the woman I had seen on the highway and learned that her name was Marcaria. She was thirty-five years old and had been crawling since her childhood, a victim of polio. To her joy, she received one of the chairs. Recipients for the other chairs were located quickly. I found three beggars on the street who were scooting around using their hands on makeshift skateboards. When I asked them if they'd like a wheelchair, of course they said yes. We gave away the twenty-two chairs, but people kept coming.

I pondered Proverbs 21:13, which states, "Whoso stoppeth his ears at the cry of the poor, he also shall cry himself, but shall not be heard." I felt the Lord was speaking to me, giving me the opportunity to help others. My experience in the States showed me that the wheelchairs were out there. The task was to get them to Guatemala and to the people in such dire need. I made up my mind I was going to do it. I didn't know how. I really didn't have a clue. I promised those who had not received wheelchairs that I would do my best. I asked them to pray and promised I'd return in six months. I fulfilled my promise, and throughout the years, went back again and again as the people kept praying.

As an American, it's hard to describe the amount of joy and freedom these wheelchairs gave these individuals. From a life of constant struggle, literally living in the dirt and relying on others for all needs, to a life of mobility was truly a gift of new life! Without a wheelchair, they could not move about their community, go to church, or work without the constant help of others. Family members often transported them in wheelbarrows or on their backs. Not only did these wheelchairs bless the recipients, but it freed their family members as well. The wheelchair gave independence and opportunities formerly never considered. I will never forget the joy in the faces of the recipients, as well as in those of their families and friends. This encouraged me to do all in my power to bring more hope and joy to these children of God. What a blessing it was to see these poor, disabled people start to shine out of joy as we lifted them up on their new chairs. Many had no legs or were deformed from birth and had spent most of their lives either crawling around in the dirt from place to place or simply never leaving their house. This rewarding experience far outweighed the trials of our journey down to Guatemala. Proverbs 31:20 states, "...he stretcheth out her hand to the poor; yea, she reacheth forth her hands to the needy." By demonstrating Christ's love in a meaningful way, we provided our own testimony to the villagers.

In a nearby village, we took a wheelchair to a fifty-four-year-old woman who had been confined to her bed for the past twelve years and could go nowhere because of a severe case of arthritis. The entire family was so grateful that they gave us their only rooster, which we reluctantly accepted so as not to offend them. We soon discovered that the rooster conveniently eliminated the need for an alarm clock, as he joyfully woke us each morning around 5:00 a.m. Blessings returned!

Sandy was nearing the end of her pregnancy at this time, close to giving birth to Matthew. We were living on the farm in Guatemala and fortunately Sandy's doctor was at the best private hospital in Guatemala City, within a mile of the U.S. embassy. He had practiced for six years at Mayo Clinic in Minnesota. Sandy had a great experience and was treated like a queen. We recalled Michael's birth in Florida and the complications. In looking back, I again wondered how a different outcome of his birth might have changed my calling in life. Would I have been the father of a boy with cerebral palsy instead of, or in addition to, bringing wheelchairs to thousands?

In 1989, when Matthew was about six months old, Sandy took him back to the States to visit family. I took the opportunity with Mickey (Michael) to travel. We took the bus to Puerto Barrios on the Atlantic Coast and a boat to Belize in order to visit old Mennonite friends. We met up with Craig Boyer, whom I had worked with at Caribbean Light and Truth Mission. He was from upstate New York and had joined a conservative Mennonite church. Craig came down to be a short-term missionary and ended up marrying one of the Mayan pastor's daughters. We went by boat to Punta Gorda and took a bus to Blue Creek. There we met Craig who took us to Santa Cruz. Craig was one of the people that had come with us when we found Uxbenka, one of the Mayan Ruins. Now he lived within a mile of the ruins.

Craig was coming back from some church meetings in Blue Creek. We drove home with him, and as soon as we got there, we found a community-based health worker who had been waiting. A man had been bitten by a yellow jaw (fer-de-lance) and needed his help. This was the same type of snake I'd found under my backpack in the jungle five years before. Craig went to Santa Elena, a village five miles west, leaving Michael and me at his house with his wife Flor and their kids. When Craig came rushing back through, I jumped in the pickup to help take the wounded man to the hospital. The British Army had a doctor with anti-venom medication about an hour away west of Punta Gorda, and it was our intention to take him there. The injured man and two of his friends who had come with us changed our course as we drove as fast as we could towards the British doctor. They refused to go to the British doctor and instead wanted to go to a bush doctor. We got to the "T" in the road and were instructed to go to the bush doctor at Big Creek, who was in the opposite direction of the British doctor, to whom I felt we should bring him. I protested all the way and kept telling Craig to just take him to the British doctor. Craig explained that if we took him to the British doctor and he didn't live, they would hold him responsible.

We got to the bush doctor, but he didn't have the herbs he needed to treat him so he sent us to another bush doctor near Punta Gorda. Following his directions, we took off and drove right past the entrance to the British doctor. I had a hard time with that. Soon, we found the bush doctor who calmly took the patient and started treating him. The man had been bitten on the hand and by the time we got there, the floorboard in the cab of the pickup where he'd been sitting was full of coagulated blood. The doctor took off the tourniquet and gave him some roots to chew on, some different herbs to drink, and a poultice of jungle leaves and herbs to draw out the poison. Immediately, the screaming man, who was Kekchi-Mayan, came to his senses and started explaining, through a translator, what had happened. This snake's venom causes excruciating pain, and it had bitten him after he'd crossed a river and was reaching up to pull himself out of the water. We asked the bush doctor how he knew what to do, and he shared with us that his grandfather was from Nicaragua and had passed down the secrets of the jungle herbs to him. The man survived, and I became a firm believer in alternative medicine.

While we were with the snake-bitten man, Michael had been left behind in the jungle house with Flor. Michael thoroughly enjoyed the afternoon. Flor was bathing her kids in a stream, so he joined in!

From December 1989 to February 1990, for a small fee, we were able to rent a house that belonged to a missionary family, the Jacksons, who were on a three-month furlough. During that time, two days a week I went back to the farm to train Amilcar who was from the Mennonite church and who eventually became responsible for the farm. Throughout the years, we have kept in contact with him and his family. His sister-in-law, Lucinda, now cooks and cleans for the wheelchair factory and the guesthouse. The farm was a chicken ranch for ten years. Once the war was over, Melvin donated it to the Mennonite church. I had an option to buy it, but we didn't because it was too stressful for our family. At that time in the country's history, life was volatile and you never knew when armed men might show up at the farm. I wanted to buy it, but Sandy wanted to move back to the States with our boys.

As an example, on February 3, 1990 at 7:15 in the morning, we were on our way to have a Bible study and picnic with missionary friends. We were going to pick them up in Pastores, and then drive for three hours to Lake Atitlan. On the road, just inside the village, we passed two vehicles strangely parked on either side of the road. We were stopped and ordered to get out with our hands up by the guerillas in the vehicles. They frisked me and told my dad, Michael, and me to walk further up the road where there were already about a hundred people being forced to listen to a propaganda speech. Sandy was guarded back at the van with Matthew. We later learned that forty to fifty guerillas were in Pastores, all heavily armed with M16s, hand grenades, and rocket launchers. Prayers were fervent! After a long forty-five minutes of waiting, we began hearing machine gun fire. The guerrilla that was speaking suddenly said, "Tenemos problemas (we have problems)," and he took off through the crowd, leaving us to escape. While the gunfire continued, many hid under cars, behind walls or trees, and any other place that seemed safe and out of the way. Eventually, we learned the army had arrived from the other side of the village and disrupted the temporary control that the guerrillas had taken over the village.

As Sandy saw us approach the van upon we return, she reached for Michael expecting to need to comfort his fears but instead, found him laughing with excitement, thinking he was participating in the biggest game of "hide and seek" ever. No time was wasted in getting the van turned around in about a twenty-foot space, and we headed back to Antigua.

Later that evening, we went back to Pastores to find out if the Youngs, our Christian friends who lived there, were hurt. Prayers were answered when we found them safe at their home. They shared how the gunfire had continued off and on throughout the day, but miraculously, there were no injuries. The community, again, benefitted from the powerful prayers of the faithful. "Hear my voice, O God, in my prayer: preserve my life from fear of the enemy." (Psalm 64:1)

CHAPTER 12

GROWING WITH GRACE

n 1990, I was feeling very discouraged and sad, thinking the Lord was through using me in Guatemala. Our two-year commitment would be up on the first of March, and we were supposed to head back to the States. I didn't like the idea of returning to a country so "full" after living in one so poverty-stricken. "…the harvest truly is great, but the laborers are few." (Luke 10:2b) Apparently, the Lord saw my heart because doors began to open, little by little.

One of our visitors at this time was Carl DuRocher. Carl had helped get the used wheelchairs for us to bring down in the fall of 1988. Carl himself was a wheelchair user and had just made plans to come and see us, a huge step of faith for the difficult travel he would endure. He not only wanted to visit Guatemala, but he had the dream of continuing to get used wheelchairs donated for the physically disabled in this desperate country. At the same time, the Lord was dealing with the Young's in Pastores to work with the afflicted and widows.

When we joined them in a discussion of starting a relief ministry, they responded with excitement and willing hearts.

As a result, the Guatemalan Relief and Craft Export (GRACE) ministry was born with the Young's, Carl and me. GRACE included the acquisition and dispersal of used wheelchairs to the physically disabled, as well as aiding the country's impoverished weavers by continuing to develop the craft export business. Many of the weavers were widowed or disabled. In addition, the Young's began seeking land to buy, which they would use to develop a community for both groups.

I was able to visit some folks who had received wheelchairs from us a couple of years before. These grateful recipients were not only happy; they were still tearfully amazed and grateful that strangers would care so much. We took great delight in being the hands and feet of Jesus to these precious souls. The wheelchairs not only changed their lives but the lives of those who loved and cared for them as well.

In March 1990, we moved back to the United States. We landed in Cottage Grove, Wisconsin, where I had previously lived in 1968. Jobs were hard to find. I was able to help my brother Chad do some remodeling on his house for a few weeks, but within a month, we were heading to Ohio. We had some friends in Alliance who were remnants of the Fairmount Fellowship. One of the couples that had been in the traveling ministry, Andrew and Deborah Neal, were living there. Deb had just been diagnosed with cancer, making our decision to move even clearer. Andrew brought a school bus to Wisconsin, and we loaded it up and moved to Ohio.

I found a job with a carpenter who was remodeling a house owned by Phil Norcom. Phil was Jacob Meandel's son-in-law and had a large wholesale greenhouse. Phil's shipping manager was in the reserves and got called to service in the summer of 1990, heading to Iraq as part of Desert Storm. I ended up getting hired as the shipping manager for Phil's greenhouse. Even before I was working for Phil, he had let us use an empty greenhouse, which he used to store wheelchairs. By the time he needed to use the warehouse, his brother-in-law had found an empty warehouse in nearby Sebring to store the wheelchairs. We were making contacts in the Cleveland, Akron, and Youngstown areas, looking for used wheelchairs. We would pick up the chairs, and when we had enough, drive them down to Guatemala.

In that winter of 1989–1990, we had made a promise to bring more wheelchairs down. I have always been very careful about telling someone I was going to do something, like when we were working with the weavers. If I said it, I would do it. Those who live in poverty in developing countries experience broken promises all the time. Often, people down on mission trips mean well but make promises they cannot keep, committing to something they think they'll do for those they've come to serve when they get back home. This also makes it hard for the long-term missionaries who then must do damage control, rebuilding the trust, which has been lost.

We started out in Momostenango, a municipality in the Totonicapán department. This was a natural, first place for us to focus on. We knew people who lived there from my time in the early '80s when I worked with the families that wove the wool blankets and rugs.

The ministry had grown to the point where we needed a more systematic way to identify people who needed wheelchairs. We started developing the formal process of finding and documenting the people who would receive the wheelchairs, which evolved into the system we use today. The Youngs owned an old Commodore computer, and together, we developed the application for those requesting wheelchairs. We pretty much pioneered this, as far as I know. We traveled through the area using the relationships we had and asked people to take us to those they knew who needed a chair so we could fill out the application. On this first quest through the area, we acquired about twenty applications. To have a backup plan, we threw the ball in their court. I told the applicants and their family members they should pray that we would be able to come back in six months with their wheelchairs. This helped to develop their faith and realize that this gift of a chair was truly from the Lord, using our human hands. "And all things, whatsoever ye shall ask in prayer, believing, ye shall receive." (Matthew 21:22)

One of the largest wheelchair factories in the world, Invacare, was located nearby in Elyria, Ohio. I didn't know that fact when we moved there; it was just all in God's plan. I went to Invacare and knocked on their door. I just kept asking, like the neighbor in Luke who wouldn't stop asking for bread. Jesus taught us, "…I tell you, even though he will not get up and give you the bread because of friendship, yet because of your shameless audacity he will surely get up and give you as much as you need." (Luke 11:8, NIV) By 1993, I finally got ahold of the engineer in charge of their recycling program and started a productive relationship with them.

Because I was the shipping manager for a greenhouse, the job was seasonal. When we were short on drivers, I made deliveries to the garden centers. About once a month, I went to Invacare, fill the now empty truck, and return with a load of wheelchairs. Phil had pediatric muscular dystrophy and walked using AFOs. He had a great deal of empathy for those struggling with mobility and was very supportive. We were given the partial use of a greenhouse, which was empty for a few months, and then later, a building, which contained old pottery in Sebring, Ohio. Jacob's other son, Matthew, was in the salvage business and went to bat for us by soliciting the owner for use of part of the building. In the back half, they allowed us to store the wheelchairs. About every six months, we would load up and head down to Guatemala.

Andrew was going to let us use his school bus on the first trip in July 1990, but there were only twenty wheelchairs slated to go. It was late in the gardening season so instead, our friend Chuck Wimberly let us use his half-ton cargo van. We put the wheelchairs, walkers, and crutches in the back and lay a mattress over the seat right behind the driver's seat so we could take turns sleeping as we went down. I had done repairs on these wheelchairs before we loaded them up. I took a month off work and left with Andrew, his son Joshua, and Judy Roberts. Judy was the friend who, two years before, had come down to Guatemala for three months to help Sandy before Matt was born. Judy was also the granddaughter of Rufus Sherrill who had been instrumental in connecting Jim Roberts to The House of Jesus revival in the winter of 1970–1971. We had barely enough money to get down there, but just before we left, Phil surprised us with a generous donation. By the time we made it to Guatemala, we had experienced a couple of breakdowns. Without Phil's financial help, we would have been in trouble.

We had our list of recipients. We went to each one of them and gave away the wheelchairs. Six months earlier, before moving back to the States, we had rented a small facility in Momostenango. We had brought some sewing machines, which were donated by ladies in a Lutheran church and hired Flora, a Mayan girl who had experience in a sewing factory. We set up a workshop to do repairs on the wheelchairs, and then we trained locals how to fix the chairs. Flora helped us set up and run the sewing school. All but one of our workers were in wheelchairs. We brought down material with the initial intent of taking the finished crafts back to the States, but new import laws made it next to impossible. Instead, they made products they could sell locally like aprons and potholders.

We soon identified another twenty people who needed wheelchairs, and I again asked them and their families for prayer that doors would open for me to return in six months. The next winter, I was able to put wheelchairs on a bus leaving from Indiana and going to Guatemala. I used one of the greenhouse trucks and drove the chairs to Indiana.

Then came the day when we were able to buy our own transportation, a 1971 GMC school bus with a diesel motor. I had a lot of friends from the Alliance Christian Center with many useful skills. Kurt Klingelhoffer and other friends from church helped to rehabilitate and modify the bus. David Walker, who owned a painting business, painted it light blue and Kurt welded a rack on the top of the bus. It was about 7x19 feet, so we could carry forty-five wheelchairs on the top of the bus. Joe Sukoz did the metal work. We turned it into a camper by building sleeping bunks and adding a table. We left about six of the seats intact so it was comfortable for twelve people to travel.

We loaded the wheelchairs and drove down in July 1991. We left from the parking lot of the Christian Alliance Center. Everyone gathered to pray for us and then saw us off. We towed a high top van down to donate to a hospital in Antigua. This van was donated by the widow of a man who had died after many years in a wheelchair. The hospital would use this van as an ambulance. We later received a picture of the van dedication with the first lady of Guatemala present. This would have never been possible without the help of the Kurt and Sally Jackson family. They were, and are, an example of sold-out missionaries who have given their lives to serve the poor. I have received so much wisdom from them in how not to be a "fair-weather missionary."

We took off optimistically but broke down in Arkansas, much like our breakdown three years earlier with the first load. This bus had a six-cylinder diesel engine, and for some reason, there was no stabilizer piece to keep the injection tubes from vibrating, so we cracked one of the injection lines. We were on the off ramp in Hope, Arkansas that Sunday morning when a guy came by on his way to church and stopped. He was a teacher and one of his former students had a welding shop, so he brought the part there to get it brazed. While that was getting done, Tom McCune found a radiator hose on the side of the interstate. He showed it to me, and I told him to throw it under the driver's seat.

Tom and Julie had made this into a family mission trip and brought all four of their children along. They had been part of The Assembly back in the mid 1970s with us. They had spent time in Mexico about the same time I was in the Chihuahua State Penitentiary. After about a half-year there, they picked up a lot of Spanish, which would prove instrumental in their ministry.

Our next incident involved a flat tire in Texas. While getting it fixed, we realized that the used tires at the gas station were better than the tire we were getting fixed. While we were waiting, a guy from a landscaping business showed up. After telling him about our mission, he was so impressed that he pulled out his wallet and paid for one of the used tires to be put on so we could trash the flat one.

We had forty-five wheelchairs but requests for only twenty. After getting through Mexico, we started praying about the extras. We were driving through Quetzaltenango, the second largest city in Guatemala, and saw a sign for the Verbo church. Verbo means "the Word." We went in and talked to the missionaries, telling them we had wheelchairs to give away. They owned a radio station, so they took us to the station to announce the opportunity. We went to Momostenango to deliver the twenty wheelchairs we had promised, which took about three days.

During this time, we also visited the sewing school and the repair shop. We met a schoolteacher who had heard about us. She was from one of the small mountain communities and had come to tell us about Abram, an eight-year-old boy who crawled to school every day. The teacher was very impressed with this little boy who wanted to learn so desperately. We drove up to his village and gave him a wheelchair. It was an adult chair—way too big for him, but it's all we had. This was another frustrating situation for us, not having a pediatric chair, which this child needed. Abram, however, was delighted.

We went back to Verbo Church and gave the rest of the wheelchairs to them. We unloaded them in the church, along with the commodes, walkers, and crutches that were left over. By this time, it was getting easier to predict the ways of the Lord. We gave them all away. Amazingly, the number of people who came for the equipment matched exactly the quantity and type of equipment we had to give.

When we were back in Antigua, near Guatemala City, we met up with Melvin Kiepfer. Melvin, the founder of the boys' farm we had built and managed from March 1988 to March 1990. We needed to deliver a trailer to a buyer in Texas. This was the same fifth wheel trailer we had brought from Pennsylvania three years before. He drove the mission truck and caravanned with us back to the States.

On the second day of our trip, we were near the Isthmus of Mexico. This is a very desolate area. The road is narrow, with one lane each way, and it has no shoulder. About a half-hour before dark, the radiator hose on Melvin's truck sprung a leak. Along this stretch of road, there are miles of nothing. With it getting dark and with no shoulder on the road, we were quite concerned. He was stuck in the one lane, blocking it for any other traffic, which might show up. Tom recalled the radiator hose he had found on the road in Arkansas. We pulled it out from under the seat, modified it, and put it on. We didn't have water in the vehicles, but miraculously, there was a little pond by the road, the only one for miles and miles we later learned. It worked and we were on our way! Considering the danger and desolation of the area, and with darkness coming soon, the breakdown in Arkansas was revealed as yet another divine intervention in the Lord's care for us.

In 1 Corinthians 13:12, we are reminded, "For now we see through a glass, darkly; but then face to face: now I know in part; but then shall I know even as also I am known." This was another reminder to always trust in the Lord through life's difficulties. You never know when what looks like a problem might become a blessing!

The more wheelchairs we gave away, the more we realized how much we didn't know. Wheelchairs can and should be fitted to the individual in order to provide the proper support. Ill-fitting wheelchairs can create pressure ulcers. We were trying to work with some clinics, but at this point, we operated by word of mouth from families, caregivers, neighbors, and medical professionals. We continued to seek a better way to serve those who received the wheelchairs.

Six months later, in June 1992, we had a physical therapist and a wheelchair seating specialist fly down to meet us. Patrick Rimke worked as a seating specialist for a wheelchair company in Akron, Ohio called Akron-Cleveland Home Medical Services. Years later, Patrick would become the director of Wheels Of Hope. Patrick and his wife Lynda went to church in Kent, Ohio with Kurt, so they were well aware of our needs. The other volunteer, a physical therapist from Wisconsin, was a friend of Carl's. They both came to help us with seating and positioning.

On this trip, I drove down with Sandy, Michael, and Matthew. Michael was four and a half years old and Matthew was turning three on this trip. My brother, Denny, had taken a bus to Brownsville, Texas and joined us. We even had our native Guatemalan German Shepherd, Loba, with us. In addition to our family, we had other volunteer drivers. After we delivered wheelchairs in Momostenango, we went to the sewing school. Near the sewing school, I saw a small girl carrying a bigger girl on her back, accompanied by an older couple. She was walking up the hill, carrying her sister from the bus station to our GRACE facility. When we gave a wheelchair to the girl, her younger sister was just as happy as she was. She had always carried her sister everywhere. That image will always stay with me—some things you never forget.

We made repairs at the shop. We were learning that Momostenango was not centrally located in the area in which we were delivering the wheelchairs, making it difficult for many to get their chairs fixed. Transportation was, and is, an issue. While traveling, we stopped at Lake Atitlan. This lake had not yet been developed and was known for its beauty, climate, and native Mayan villages. We noticed a mission team nearby, praying with a guy who had a deformity and infection in one of his feet. We walked up to them when they finished praying. I observed the situation and said, "See that bus right there? We have a pair of crutches for you!" What an honor to provide the blessing of answered prayers. These are the types of everyday occurrences the Lord uses to help others and to build faith. Don't let these go by without giving God the glory!

While driving to Chimaltenango, our radiator hose broke about a mile before we got there. Almost the second we pulled over on the side of the road, a missionary, Bill Byler, and his son, who were on their motorcycle, drove by us and saw the Ohio license plate. They pulled over and his son took Rick, one of our volunteers, into town to get a new hose. While talking, it turned out that the missionary's best friend was Bob Mullet, the Mennonite who had been my boss in Sarasota, Florida when I worked for Mullet's Windows and Doors. Both Bob and Bill were raised in the Old Order Amish in Middlefield, Ohio. Had we not had Ohio plates, would they have stopped? It's amazing how God uses relationships to weave our stories of faith and service. Having eyes that can see and understand the Lord's working in our lives builds our faith and blesses others.

The next day we stayed in Chimaltenango to give a wheelchair away. We visited some of our Mennonite friends and gave wheelchairs to a couple of elderly ladies. We also found Chito Pichya, a recipient of one of our first wheelchairs. We stopped near the park and put him in a loaner wheelchair while our team members were doing repairs on the chair he'd had for almost three years. Chito told me his dream was to have his own wheelchair repair shop, so that got the ball rolling. We started the plans to transfer the repair shop to Chimaltenango and train Chito. The location was much more central to the area where we were working. In addition, it was along the Pan-American Highway and within thirty-five miles of Guatemala City. He is still running the shop we set up there. He's fixed thousands of wheelchairs.

Kurt Klingelhoffer had been uncomfortable with us driving that bus down with such bad tires after the first trip. He had a truck with good tires on it and basically swapped out the wheels so we weren't driving on bald tires. One of the drivers who came with us was a truck driver and mechanic—Rick Peters, from Minnesota. Rick and Kurt decided it would be a good idea to bring an extra canister for the air brakes. With air brakes, if one goes out all of the brakes freeze up.

On our way back to the States on that second trip, the civil war was still going on. It would be four years before the peace accord was signed, so there was still a lot of guerilla activity in Guatemala. Down along the southern Pan-American Highway there was a temporary bridge because the original one had been blown up. This is where the canister on one of the brakes went out, and we were stuck in a very dangerous place an hour before dark. Rick managed to pull the truck off the road, and he was able to put the spare canister on before it got dark. Being stranded on the side of the road would have been very dangerous, and we praised the Lord for the foresight, generosity, and skills of those who cared for us.

This wheelchair ministry was definitely a calling. Unlike answering a ministry advertisement where the position and goals are clearly laid out, God showed me the work we were to do one step at a time. Tom, the guy who had found the radiator hose on the first trip, was a member of a Pentecostal church and was always inviting us to come and worship with them. The night we went, they had a prophet visiting. Halfway through the service, the prophet pointed me out and yelled with conviction, "You've got a calling!" I felt confirmed.

CHAPTER 13

NEW HARVEST

I n 1992, my work captured the attention of Joni and Friends Ministries (JAF)—an organization founded and lead by Joni Eareckson Tada, which I mentioned briefly earlier in this book. Joni was, and is, an internationally known disability advocate, author, radio host, mouth-artist, and conference speaker. Joni is a quadriplegic as the result of a diving accident when she was seventeen years old. Through trusting in Jesus, she was able to accept God's will in her life and is living a life filled with ministry for all, but specifically focusing JAF on the disability community.

JAF's Director of Field Ministry Conrad Mandsager had a young son who was a quadriplegic after a fall from bed and knew well the challenges of getting the right wheelchair and other related equipment to meet his unique needs. As Conrad's garage began to fill with wheelchairs and other durable medical equipment, which his son had outgrown, he wondered how he could get that equipment to those who could use it.

One of JAF's programs, the Christian Fund for the Disabled, had revealed thousands in the United States could not access or upgrade equipment because they were underinsured or uninsured. Conrad developed the Wheels for the World (WFW) concept as a solution to both issues. First, WFW put back into service usable wheelchairs and other durable medical equipment, which were piling up in garages and back rooms across America. Second, they provided this equipment to those who could not access it through the traditional means of public or private insurance. Unfortunately, JAF's attorneys raised concerns about the liability exposure of distributing used equipment in the U.S. Discouraged after months of trying to resolve the liability issues in the U.S. market, Conrad redirected the new program toward the even greater needs in the developing countries of the global south.

I partnered with JAF, agreeing that all GRACE activity would from then on be known as Wheels for the World (WFW). The ministry was self-supporting, relying on the generosity of donors. By spring 1993, I had already returned to Guatemala. We had bought three Mercedes trucks, two twelve-ton and one fifteen-ton. We filled them with wheelchairs and four of us took turns driving. Melvin Kiepfer joined us with a Toyota pickup, driving from Ontario, Canada and rendezvousing with us in central Ohio. Fortunately, it was an uneventful trip. While I was dealing with the Guatemalan customs paperwork on the trucks, my teammates had already found and fitted a man with a wheelchair. We worked with Kurt Jackson and his First Steps Outreach Ministries. This ministry had a facility that used to house mission teams. This facility was a great resource for organizations, like WFW, which brought teams of volunteers for wheelchair distributions.

Soon after arriving, I went to find Marcaria, the woman who had inspired my work. Unfortunately, the shack she had been living in was moved. We spoke to the mayor and received permission to build her a house. With some lumber and tin from the temporary truck shelving system, as well as help from Kurt Jackson, we built her a 15x15 square foot house. Compared to the termite-infested dwelling she had left, it was a mansion. Her poverty was extreme. She would collect pieces of plastic from the dump to add to her meager supply of firewood to cook her tortillas. Blessing her with a new home brought joy to her life and eased some of her suffering. In addition, Kurt Jackson was able to get her a wood cook stove, modified to sit close to the ground. Even with a wheelchair, she continued to crawl in her house and just used the wheelchair for travel.

For the second time I was able to get an audience with the First Lady of Guatemala, Magda de Serrano. During an earlier visit we had given her twenty wheelchairs. She had quickly given them away and was immediately swamped with hundreds of requests. She had been able to get over one hundred wheelchairs from China and was seeking more. The blessing of serving the poor is contagious. Jesus said, "It is more blessed to give than to receive." (Acts 20:35b) The hearts of the president and his wife were in the Lord's hand and the country was blessed. Unfortunately, on this trip we learned that her husband, President Jorge Serrano Elías, had been deposed from power for making a stand against corruption. They both ended up in exile in Panama.

My conviction grew. Giving wheelchairs to those with disabilities was only the first step. To be effective, the chairs needed to be properly fitted to the recipient. Now to do this, mission teams that came for the wheelchair deliveries often included physical therapists, occupational therapists, and seating specialists. In this way, each recipient was correctly fitted to the chair. Another problem was provided access for people to get their chairs repaired when either something broke or from the normal wear and tear. WFW only accepted donations of manual wheelchairs, which they refurbished in an effort to provide a chair that would last a long time, not one that needed batteries or electricity like a power-chair would require.

During this trip, our team spent four days training seven people at a facility in Chimaltenango, who themselves were disabled, to repair and refurbish wheelchairs. Later that fall, the repair facility became fully operational and fully staffed, managed by Guatemalans with disabilities. Chito, the leader of the refurbishing team, became an integral part of WFW, even traveling with the teams to other locations. Chito and his team had formerly been recipients of giving. In their new positions, they now had the blessing of being the givers. What joy for them to realize and use their newly developed skills and have positions of such great importance in their community!

Wheels for the World continued to expand. By October 1993, we had distributed over 250 wheelchairs to people in Nicaragua, Honduras, and Guatemala. Other targeted areas included Ghana, Romania, Russia, Poland, and Vietnam. Our focus was to not only meet the need for wheelchairs, but to meet an even greater need: the need for Christ. Evangelism was always the focus on every distribution trip. We tried to include local pastors in our distributions. Our goal was to educate pastors who taught that sin caused disabilities. In John 9:3, Jesus addressed this issue. "Jesus answered, Neither hath this man sinned, nor his parents: but that the works of God should be made manifest in him."

I continued to reconnect with people previously served, occasionally by providing new equipment for growing children. Stories of poverty abounded, fueling our passion for serving the Lord in this ministry. In Nicaragua, we met a widow who had both legs amputated. To move around, she sat in one box, pushed another other box in front of her, climbed out of the first box and into the other, and then repeated the process.

Another time, I was in a Mayan village five hours from Guatemala City. I learned about a woman who lived in the country, one in need of a wheelchair. When I arrived, I found a tiny, dark, one-room hut. Maria, a young woman who had contracted polio in 1976 and had been bedridden in the hut since she was twenty-one years old, greeted me. When I carried her into the sunlight and placed her gently in her wheelchair, her smile could not be contained. Maria had not been able to leave her hut and move around her community—now another to whom new life was given.

As the teams continued to serve, getting the communities' pastors involved became a vital component of the distributions. The local pastors often presented the wheelchair recipients with a Bible and shared the gospel with them. I became passionate about using the local pastors and allowing them to do what God had called them to do—share the gospel. Many people accepted Christ over the years, and their pastors were living among them. The pastors discipled the new believers and encouraged them to participate in worship. This supported a life-long faith journey for these new Christians, living and fellowshipping in a community of faith with their friends and family. Convincing pastors to get involved was not always easy, but we did get many to see this as a calling to reach the unreached.

As mission trips increased, I saw the profound impact these trips made on the people serving on the teams. A phrase from the Don Francisco song, "The Proof," described my heart quite clearly. To paraphrase, it says, the proof of God is in the hands of those who are moved by His Spirit. My heart was in this service to the Lord not just in word, but also in deed.

One of the issues, which became apparent quite early, was the need for pediatric wheelchairs. In early 1996, Joni spoke on her radio show and told Abram's story as an example of the desperate need. Unfortunately, his situation was not rare, and the teams had come across many children who could so greatly benefit from a wheelchair that fit.

Many developing countries had been manufacturing wheelchairs for years, but in 1996, very few of them were pediatric wheelchairs. I could give many examples of adults who had crawled or been bed-bound for their entire childhood because of the lack of pediatric chairs. Unfortunately, seventy-five to eighty percent of WFW's donations were adult chairs. WFW started a concerted push to find and distribute pediatric chairs.

There are certain people in life who are truly inspiring. Dr. Mike Francis was, and is, one of those for me. Mike was a visionary regarding the changing missionary movement. He was one of the first to talk about the importance of developing local pastors versus bringing in a missionary from the United States. Mike had a good friend, a Vietnamese pastor whose name was Ming Deng, who lived in Ohio. In 1992, Mike and Ming had learned about Wheels for the World through their church, The Chapel, so they came to visit. Mike had polio as a child and spent a year and a half at home recovering. It didn't leave him disabled, but it left him compassionate for those who were. He was a man of modest means and had been an army doctor in Korea during the Vietnam War. God put him in my life to mentor me and see the value of relationship in ministry. He often used the term "friendship evangelism." It really made me think about how I interacted with people and helped to mold my ministry. He came to meet me and quickly became one of my most treasured friends. Mike's a passionate thinker. He immediately started brainstorming how to get the gospel out with the wheelchairs.

Pastor Deng had told Mike about the need in his country. He had pictures of hospitals where there were three patients in a single bed. The Vietnamese doctors thought nothing of it. Only twenty years before, their field hospitals had been in caves, which were basically tunnels with patients in hammocks. Compared to the caves, this was a major improvement. Vietnam quickly became another targeted country for our ministry, with our dream of taking wheelchairs to those in need.

In 1994, when I was working for Joni and Friends, Hope Haven (HH) in Rock Valley, Iowa agreed to underwrite half of the budget for Wheels For the World. Hope Haven had spent over thirty years helping people with disabilities in Iowa and was in the process of expanding their ministry internationally. Our third son, Ben, had been born in Alliance, Ohio on January 7th. I accepted the position, and Sandy, our three sons, and I moved to Iowa to start the program that was to be called Hope Haven International (HHI). I became a shared employee with Hope Haven and Joni and Friends' Wheels For the World.

Wheels For the World had been built on volunteers. Volunteers collected the chairs, raised money, unloaded the trucks, and refurbished the wheelchairs. I could get volunteers, wheelchairs, and equipment, but I wasn't great at raising money. Personally, I felt like I didn't look the part with my beard and "relaxed attire." When I spoke about getting wheelchairs to people, I used pictures that showed the need, which no one doubted. I also spoke about the crude living conditions we experienced to get the wheelchairs to people. I wasn't one to shy away from sacrifice. I found that many people wanted to give money and come but only if they could be flown down in comfort, stay in a nice hotel, see the sights—like a tourist. Our goal was to use any money we raised as efficiently as possible in order to get the most wheelchairs to the most people. This involved a rather "bare bones" trip which was not acceptable to many.

When I transferred to Rock Valley in November, I did so with the understanding that I needed to continue with two of my projects—my new commitment to Vietnam and the ministry I had started in Guatemala. Nor would I desert the dedicated volunteers in Ohio.

So in Ohio, we put some folks on staff and left Patrick Rimke in charge. In later years, Joni and Friends decided to exclusively use inmates to refurbish wheelchairs, so they dropped Patrick's organization. They decided to rename their ministry "Wheels of Hope" after the title of the Readers Digest article that came out in May 1997. We remained good partners over the years, but their focus shifted to northern Thailand.

At that time, Hope Haven International was focused on the Dominican Republic and Romania. Back in 1990, the attention of the world went to Romania when it was discovered they were warehousing people with physical and mental disabilities in some of the worst institutions imaginable. In response to many nations' condemnations, Romania developed a ministry of the handicapped and requested help from the outside world. Hope Haven was one of those invited to come into the country. HH had been an international leader in providing vocational training and job opportunities for people with developmental disabilities for many years. Included in that delegation was Senator Mike Menning, a Minnesota state senator. Mike had a son who was born with microcephaly and was deeply interested in the care and rights of people with disabilities. He was also Chairman of the Board for Joni and Friends and had helped to provide a connection for me from JAF to HH. When I came to HH, they had already been sending teams to Romania for years.

Hope Haven hired a couple from Cokato, Minnesota to move to Romania. He was a farmer, married to a Romanian woman. Missionaries David & Mariana Nyquist moved to Romania to have an in-country presence in deliver wheelchairs and evangelize. Some wheelchairs were refurbished in Romania by staff and other wheelchair users. Staff member, Daniel Mereuta eventually became the director of Portul Sperantei (Hope Haven in Romania). Daniel has now been its director for the past eighteen years. He has overseen the distribution of more than 10,000 wheelchairs in the country.

In the early 1990s, one of HH's board members was visiting his daughter who was a missionary in the Dominican Republic. One Sunday morning, in a rural area, he got into a mission van to go to the church. A mother came to the van with her handicapped daughter. He held this little girl on his lap all of the way to church. It troubled him that she didn't have a wheelchair. About a week later, when he was back in Rock Valley, he walked into HH's Executive Director David Vanningan's office, pointed his finger at David and said, "We gotta' do something about this." HH later went down and made contact with the Dominican Rehabilitation Association and started opening doors for HHI. The first shipment of wheelchairs was sent out a month after my coming to HH in late 1994. The first wheelchair in the Dominican Republic was delivered to a young man named Franklin. Since then, nearly 3,000 wheelchairs have been distributed to those in need in the country.

Around 1993, KLM AirLines was celebrating their seventy-fifth anniversary. They had a "bridging the world" contest in which the grand prizewinner would receive twenty-five free tickets to fly anywhere with free air cargo. Joni submitted and won! We prepared one hundred wheelchairs in Rock Valley, Iowa and took them to the Northwest air cargo site in Sioux Falls, South Dakota to ship to Ghana. This was in the spring, and Sandy and I had just bought a house two blocks from Hope Haven. Unfortunately, our closing date coincided with the trip, so I asked Joni if Paul Dykshoorn could take my seat. Paul was one of the pastors from the Alliance Christian Center who helped us get organized, as well as raised funds for the new Wheels For the World ministry.

When we arrived in Iowa, WFW had just done a wheelchair drive in Oklahoma City, and a semi load of wheelchairs was waiting for us in Rock Valley. The owners of an empty Pioneer seed corn facility agreed to let us store them there. Eventually, a tractor supply company also gave us some space. We started training volunteers. When we moved to Iowa, we bought an old Mercedes twelve-in-a-half-ton, twenty-six-foot truck. We moved our personal things, as well as twenty-five wheelchairs, ready to go in boxes. Almost immediately, an opportunity arrived for us to get these wheelchairs on a UPS truck to New Orleans where they'd be put on The Caribbean Mercy, one of the Mercy Ships. Within a week or two, the first shipment was off to the Dominican Republic. It took us close to a year to get a shipment to Vietnam, but in January 1996, Hope Haven International delivered wheelchairs to Vietnam. I was still a shared employee with JAF.

This was an exciting time for me. I was given a lot of decision-making power and was able to react to God's movements and guidance. Rather than sitting in meetings with a board, restricted by our human sight and vision, I was allowed to respond to a myriad of divine interventions and provisions that continued to lead me as our ministry grew.

In 1995, my first full year with HHI, we were blessed with an unexpected gift. Our religious service coordinator, Pastor Bill Van Dyken, was speaking in a church in Sioux Falls, South Dakota. After the service, the deputy director of the Department of Corrections came up to talk to him. At that time, the governor of South Dakota was trying to incorporate community service work for inmates, with the possibility of sentence reduction in some cases. Within no time, we had set up a wheelchair shop and developed a partnership with an organization working in the prison near Sioux Falls called the West Prison Farm, which was a medium-security facility. We started refurbishing wheelchairs in the barn at the farm. The prison farm was in transition from being a productive working farm to becoming a vocational youth school. Within a year we moved to the South Dakota State Penitentiary in Sioux Falls.

We started out in the old prison industry building and were there for our first five years. About fifteen years ago, they built a modern, 18,000-square-foot building in the courtyard. HHI had and continues to have close to forty percent of it, which is around 8,000 square feet. They run a machine shop, carpentry shop, sewing and refurbishing shop, and do wheelchair manufacturing. They provide the supervision, tools and materials, and the state pays the inmates twenty-five cents per hour. In addition, the inmates in the prison sew the upholstery and make the seating systems' headrests, footrests, seat belts, and harnesses that go to all of their eight locations. Daily, there are up to forty inmates working in the shops.

Working is a privilege and inmates want to be there. The prison administration likes this arrangement. Working is a positive incentive for the inmates and is dependent on their choices and behavior. It beats using a system where threats control behavior. Their cells are 6'x9' and shared by two inmates. They could easily spend twenty-two hours a day in their cells. To get out and work in the wheelchair shop is desirable. We have a lot of lifers working for us that will never be expelled from prison, but the ones who do eventually leave are learning valuable skills and a strong work ethic, which they can choose to use in society outside of the prison. We also have a shop in Sioux Falls on Kiwanis Avenue. Many of our workers there are from the trustee unit. We pick them up every day, and they box the wheelchairs and prepare the loads to be shipped overseas. They also load parts, which support the other shops. It's been a good program.

We brought in extra trustees one day to unload a semi-trailer of donations. After we finished, I was talking to the guys, and it didn't take long to realize that one of them, Simon, was with his mother and sisters at our reunion with members of the traveling ministry in Indiana fifteen years before. His parents traveled with us back in the mid-70s when we brought the first load of chairs to Guatemala. Simon had gotten mixed up in drugs and ended up doing time in prison. Had we not asked the right questions, we would have never known of this connection.

We can accomplish what we accomplish because of volunteers and inmates. There is a medium-security prison in Springfield, South Dakota where they're currently training inmates to work on milling machines, lathes, drill presses, and band saws. We go there about every other week to drop off raw materials while the prison takes care of the supervision of the workers and running the program. This is another valuable, good partnership with many benefits for all involved.

I had a great deal of support from Joni and Friends. My boss at JAF, Conrad Mandsager, had worked as the national director of Prison Fellowship Ministries before coming to Joni and Friends as their director of Field Ministries. Conrad also wanted to incorporate using inmates, so before he left JAF, he helped us by providing insight, experience, and support. Because we pioneered this model in South Dakota, it opened an easier path for other facilities. Joni and Friends had been working toward using prison labor and decided they weren't going to use retired volunteers anymore, instead of having the work done exclusively in prisons. This work has been a blessing to many of our inmates and has benefited our organizations. When the men are allowed to do important work blessing others, many of whom are physically less fortunate than them, it changes them. It also allows us to have access to the inmates the chaplains don't have access to, and we can be a positive influence on them. This has been a relationship we value and rely on to this day.

In 1995, my brother David helped us get a container of wheelchairs shipped to Guatemala. We had put together a team of volunteers to do a wheelchair delivery high up in the mountains of Huehuetenango. We all flew into Guatemala, having reserved a large van from one of the car rental companies. When we arrived, they had given away our van. Apparently, the United Nations election monitors had arrived, due to the recent election. The election had been close enough that a runoff vote was required, so the rental van had been given to the UN, monitors and we were stranded without a vehicle. I was able to get ahold of one of the Mennonite churches in Chimaltenango, and they loaned us their twenty-year-old van. About fifteen of us piled into the van (three with wheelchairs), and we drove up to Soloma, Huehuetenango. The last three hours were on very steep, narrow dirt roads. The wheelchairs had been delivered the day before in a truck. About an hour into the dirt road portion, the van hit a rock, and it punctured the gas tank. There was a slow stream of gas pouring out. It was already very late in the day, and this road was so narrow and steep that drivers had to honk the horn going around every corner to alert oncoming drivers. A little Toyota pickup truck with local Mayans stopped and offered to help. We figured we were pretty much stranded, but when they looked at our problem, one of the men pulled out, from behind his seat, a ball of homemade lye soap. He told us to wipe the gas tank off and broke off a piece of the soap, pressing it up against the leak. When we returned the van four days later to the Mennonite Mission, it still had not leaked again. I remembered the time fifteen years before, when I watched my Amish friends make their lye soap using lye, ashes, and lard. I never dreamed it would be such a miracle product for us. Who doesn't believe in guardian angels? This was the trip that, more than anything, inspired David to quit his job and start Wheels for Humanity. "According as his divine power hath given unto us all things that pertain unto life and godliness, through the knowledge of him that hath called us to glory and virtue..." (2 Peter 1:3)

In 1995, Dr. Mike Francis made a commitment to help us get wheelchairs to Vietnam. In order to save money, we cost-shared with International Aid out of Spring Lake, Michigan and put sixty-five wheelchairs in their forty-foot sea container. We paid our share, about one-fourth of the cost of the container. The wheelchairs were shipped to a hospital project they were working on in

Quang Tri, Vietnam. This was the province just south of the demilitarized zone, the sight of many battles in the Vietnam War. A lot of Vietnam veterans were interested in this area.

In January 1996, Philip Nguyen, Dr. Francis, two physical therapists, and I flew to Hanoi. I'll never forget into Hanoi. We could still see many bomb craters. Now years later, they are no longer visible. From Hanoi, we flew down to Hue, known as The Forbidden City. This area became well known because of the battle of Khe Sanh in January 1968. When we got off the plane, the officials from Quang Tri picked us up and took us to their hospital where many of the wheelchairs were stored. A few of these were designated for the hospital rather than individuals since they had none to use to move patients around the hospital. We hired a large bus and filled it up with the rest of the wheelchairs. We took them back down to Hue, where we gave roughly half of them away, mainly to amputees from the war.

We then drove to Danang where we did a wheelchair delivery at a church called Tin Lanh, Vietnamese for "good news." Philip's grandfather was one of the first converts in the Tin Lanh Christian Church, a church that goes back to French colonial days. Philip's grandfather later became a missionary to the Buon Ma Thuot area in the Central Highlands region of Vietnam. Buon Ma Thuot was the city where four missionaries were killed in 1968 during the Tet Offensive. In the late 1970s, his grandfather was put in a "re-education camp," which was actually a brutal concentration camp, where he was tortured and put into forced labor for being a threat to the communists. He had worked with the martyred missionaries during the war.

Today our contact in Vietnam is Dr. Song. Dr. Song was a twelve-year-old boy during the battle that left four missionaries dead when a hand grenade was thrown into their bunker. Doctor Song was hunkered down with his family and other church members between the Army of the Republic of Vietnam (the South Vietnamese regular army) camp and the North Vietnamese Army soldiers who were attacking them. They spent over a week living with bullets flying over their heads. The young Song wanted to help the wounded but his father made him stay in the bunker.

By March 1996, I decided to go full-time with Hope Haven International. Working for two organizations was complicated. Hope Haven International was a better fit for me.

CHAPTER 14

PROPAGATION

My younger brother, David, was living in California. In July 1995, he visited us the same week that we had a youth group helping in the warehouse refurbishing wheelchairs for an upcoming distribution in Poland. David was so impressed with the Wheels for the World mission that when he returned to southern California, he convinced his employer to donate some warehouse space. He called hospitals, nursing homes, and home medical companies and began collecting wheelchairs. He convinced a shipping company to provide free shipping to Guatemala. His non-profit organization, which he called Wheels for Humanity, had begun. In November, David took 130 wheelchairs to Guatemala.

In the fall of 1997, we embarked on our second trip to Vietnam. We decided to go to South Vietnam (Ho Chi Minh City), but also wanted to travel to Hue and Danang. At that time, the Vietnam airline consisted mainly of old, Russian planes. We weren't very excited about those local flights. Just months before, one of their planes had crashed in Cambodia and sixty-five of the sixty-six people on board died. We flew into Saigon (Ho Chi Minh City) and instead of flying regionally, we rented a bus and hired a driver to take us to Danang, which was a two-day drive. Halfway there we stopped at Nha Trang where the Christian Missionary Alliance had its seminary. This group represented the first evangelicals who settled there. Our contacts knew the pastor, so he met us and guided us to a hotel. While visiting with the pastor, we showed him pictures of what we were doing with the wheelchairs. Since evangelism was illegal, they had to use creative ways to evangelize. They would go up into the Montagnards of the Central Highlands to the indigenous people and offer innocent-looking activities like free haircuts. They were actually doing church planting both there and with the lepers. This was taking place in a country where less than ten percent of the population was Christian. Within that ten percent, only one percent was evangelical, while nine percent were Catholic. In contrast, among the lepers about ninety percent were Christian. We left them with a Polaroid camera and twenty empty Vietnamese wheelchair request forms and told them we'd be back within a week. We drove to Nha Trang and Hue for the wheelchair deliveries. When we came back to Nha Trang to spend the night, they handed us 196 wheelchair request forms with pictures attached. They had found more film and made many more copies of the request forms. We about fell over.

We went back to the States and wanted to ship another container to Danang to honor our commitment. Cathy Mulholland, an occupational therapist friend and supporter of ours, came to the rescue. One of her patients was the son of the CEO of Korean airlines. She made the request for us to ship 196 wheelchairs to Saigon on the airline. We received their commitment, loaded a semi, and took them to the Los Angeles airport (LAX) to be put on the Korean flight.

About two to three weeks later, in January 1997, we headed to Vietnam to complete the distribution. My brother was going to Danang with his team to do another distribution, and the Hope Haven team was going to Nha Trang. We all rendezvoused at LAX. We had bad weather, and while we were waiting, we learned the wheelchairs that we thought were in Danang and Nha Trang had not even left Los Angeles. The teams settled down to put it to the Lord in prayer. Both teams ended up going all the way to Danang, completed the deliveries there, and then took the twelve-hour train ride from Danang down to Nha Trang. As soon as we got off of the train in Nha Trang, the pastor and his wife met us with the joyous news that the wheelchairs had just arrived. The local minister of health had personally gone down to fast track them out of customs and rode in one of the trucks, which hauled them back up to Nha Trang. That was the beginning of our relationship with the church in Nha Trang. Pastor Hue ended up being our in-country representative.

On the flight back from Los Angeles, my brother sat next to a reporter for the *LA Times*. In May 1997, an article on David and the wheelchair ministries was featured in *Reader's Digest* because of that conversation. He told the reporter the story of a young lady who had made a profound impact on his life. Maria was a ten-year-old polio victim who was unable to walk. As David placed her in her first wheelchair, the look on her face assured him that it was the biggest event in her life. Eventually, WFH was headquartered in an almost 11,000-square-foot building in north Hollywood. Similar to my ministries, WFH relied mostly on volunteers and donations. With my humble guidance, David had learned to rely on the Lord for resources. When featured in *Town and Country* (June 2005, pp. 190–191), David shared with the reporter that on a monthly basis, it appears, "...we won't be able to make the rent or payroll, and then, for some miraculous reason, a check comes in." Operating on a small budget, David modeled his ministry after WFW, incorporating volunteer physical therapists, doctors, and chair mechanics into the deliveries.

In 2011, David resigned from WFH, which by then had merged with United Cerebral Palsy of Los Angeles County. It was straying from its original mission. In 2012, I helped him start Global Mobility.

Food For the Poor in Florida contacted us about getting wheelchairs to Jamaica. Food For the Poor was the largest NGO (non-governmental organization) in Jamaica and had medical people on staff. At this time, we had funding through the Hope Haven Support Foundation for the wheelchairs but no funding for the shipping and in-country delivery cost. We were getting numerous rehabilitation professionals—both therapists and rehabilitation technicians—paying their own airfare and volunteering their time. Our best partners in the country, and recipients of the chairs, were the Sir John Golding Rehabilitation Center, the

Mustard Seed homes, and the Golden Age homes. We engaged in many projects in Jamaica with Food For the Poor over the years.

We also sent used wheelchairs so that the users living in the rehabilitation center could repair chairs. Through a previous grant, they had received many tools, so we decided to use küschall USA wheelchairs exclusively. Based on the size of their shop, which limited the number of makes of wheelchairs they could work on, it made it easier for them to have a well-stocked shop of repair parts.

We did the same in Guatemala with Mulholland, in Nicaragua with Enduros, and in the Dominican Republic with Quickies. Expecting a small shop to stock all the parts of all the American manufacturers meant that they would need 10,000 different parts and a 5,000-square-foot warehouse. Over the next couple of years, we shipped over 150 used wheelchairs to them so they could use their skills and tools to do repairs on them.

A company called Metalcraft Industries in Oregon, Wisconsin was also involved in Jamaica. We were getting a lot of volunteers from them, including their rehab engineer and therapists. We tried to send mostly Metalcraft seating systems to Jamaica so they could work on them and train others. Metalcraft had a high-end seating system, which was very grow-able, adjustable, and durable.

The owners of the company, Jim and Joan Swinehart, had an interesting connection. I learned from Joan that she had belonged to Shalom Christian Church in Madison, Wisconsin. It was the same church Carl DuRocher attended, the man who helped me get the very first donated wheelchairs for Guatemala. Not only that, but this had been Denny's church before he died. This was just another one of those divine connections!

On many of our trips to Jamaica, Greg Skolaski came along. No other seating specialist/therapist has traveled with us more. He has joined us on more than fifty trips. Greg and I spent our teenage years in Madison, Wisconsin, but we never knew each other back then. For most of his career, Greg worked as an assistive technology supplier and an occupational therapist for Gundersen Lutheran Hospital in Lacrosse, Wisconsin. Greg and I met at a medical trade show where he was a trainer for Metalcraft seating. Joan introduced us and Greg started coming on trips. He is an unassuming man with a servant's heart, never wanting to bring attention to himself. Greg, as much as anyone I know, practices the Golden Rule by demonstrating love for his neighbor. It's important that we walk beside our friends who have not committed to the Lord, and not be judgmental.

Prior to one of our early Jamaica trips, a mother of third-grade twins came into my office. The twins were the stepchildren of Rick Kooistra, who was working with me at the time. Rick worked for Hope Haven International for over fifteen years, mainly supervising the South Dakota State Penitentiary wheelchair shop in Sioux Falls. Before working with us, he had been a corrections officer for ten years. His wife had encouraged their twins to follow a strategy with their allowance and the money they had earned. They learned they should give a portion, save a portion, and spend a portion. They came into my office to present the check they wanted to give. Because my son Ben was in their class, I asked them if they would mind if Ben personally presented a child with the wheelchair they were sponsoring, and then he could come and show pictures to the class. Of course they said yes! Ben and Sandy arrived in Jamaica on the second day of the distribution. We jokingly called Ben "Ben-JAM-in" while in Jamaica.

The next day, we were at one of the Mustard Seed Homes on the road to the Blue Mountains from Kingston, Jamaica. We wanted the first child that we seated to be the child who would be sponsored by the twins and given by Ben. Because we always document who gets the chairs, we wrote down his name. This child, who had severe cerebral palsy, had the last name of Richard. I had known that when the English deported the Acadians in 1755, most ended up in Louisiana, but some went to France, the Caribbean, and there was even a Richard family documented as ending up in Jamaica. Who knows, this young child could be a relative. So, the first child who Ben helped deliver a sponsored wheelchair for shared his last name!

In 1997, I was given about twenty-five requests for wheelchairs for small children in Kenya, mainly for a home called Dagarete. One of their biggest sponsors was Feed the Children out of Oklahoma City. These were very small children with various disabilities. What I typically liked to do was to single sort wheelchairs, trying not to mix different makes and models. This makes it easier for the team doing the adjustments and for follow-up and repairs. The chair that made the most sense was the KidCart wheelchair, which had recently been bought by Sunrise Medical (SM). SM offered the old inventory to Wheels for Humanity and David referred it on to us because we were better set to receive a donation from central Montana. We had the Kid Carts sent to an Ireton, Iowa shop where we trained volunteers on how to work specifically on them. These chairs were the top-selling pediatric stroller-based wheelchairs at the time.

Before I got too far on this project, I was in Atlanta at the Med Wheelchair Trade Show, and I bumped into Wayne Hanson, the former owner of KidCart. I thanked him for the donation, which amounted to roughly a semi-truck full of parts, materials, and wheelchairs. He actually had nothing to do with this, because by this time, he was no longer the owner. Wayne shared with us that in a couple of months, he was taking a family mission trip to Kenya. He was going to visit a friend of theirs who was a missionary doctor at the Tenwick hospital—a very old, well-established mission hospital in the Rift Valley. I decided to challenge Wayne. I had the twenty-five requests for the KidCarts for the children in Nairobi, Kenya, and since he was going to be in Kenya, I asked him if he would take a few days to do the fitting and adjustments for these children. I think Wayne thought I was crazy, thinking that I could get these wheelchairs there in that short amount of time. However, I had seen God work so many times before, that I knew the meeting had been too miraculous to not have God's hand in it. All I needed to do was trust, move forward, and let the Lord do the rest. The only way to get chairs to Kenya that fast was to take advantage of air cargo. So, I first reached out to the contact that had helped me get the wheelchairs to Jamaica. She really went to bat for us, with the main hurdle getting KLM Royal Dutch Airlines on board. Dozens of phone calls and over a month later, we finally received the approvals. I packaged and delivered the wheelchairs to the Sioux Falls airport. They were on their way, as space was available, to Kenya. The wheelchairs arrived on time, amazingly on the very day Wayne and his team were available to distribute them.

Wayne wasn't alone in his faithfulness. His wife, Lee, had developed a program in her youth that embraced the philosophy of "youth empowered by the Holy Spirit to reach out and care." During this time, Wayne also told me that he dreamed of using his wheelchair experience to design an inexpensive chair for the developing world.

In 1998, I was at the Wheels of Hope warehouse when Steve Sosebee, the founder and director of the Palestine Children's Relief Fund (PCRF) visited. Steve, who was from Kent, Ohio, was a photojournalist in Palestine during the first intifada. In the Palestinian context, the word intifada refers to attempts to "shake off" the Israeli occupation of the West Bank and Gaza Strip. He asked if I would help him with a project. Having previously pushed some wheelchairs through Wheels of Hope into Palestine, he wanted us to help him do a much bigger project with more focus on children. He came to the Wheels of Hope warehouse where I was visiting at the time to request wheelchairs for the many poor, disabled people living in the West Bank and Gaza. He asked me to come to Palestine to assess the needs. At that point, I had been doing quite a bit of travel in Vietnam and Latin America. With my young family, I was trying to limit the amount of time I was away from home. Steve immediately offered to pay not only my way, but Sandy's also. So in July 1999, we shipped the wheelchairs designated for Gaza.

Unfortunately, with customs delays, the wheelchairs did not arrive during the time we were there, but we were able to tour the disability organizations, hospitals, and refugee camps in the Gaza strip. We also got to spend time in Bethlehem, the Old City, and east Jerusalem. The thing that stuck out to both Sandy and me was the hospitality that the Palestinians showed to us. As our group walked through the streets of Gaza, it was obvious we were not from there. The Palestinians went out of their ways to welcome us. The impression they left on me affected how I saw refugees. From then on, I went out of my way to be friendly, kind, and always welcoming when I came across refuges. Deuteronomy 10:19 instructs, "Love ye therefore the stranger: for ye were strangers in the land of Egypt."

One of the challenges during my second trip to Gaza, eighteen months later, was manipulating all the checkpoints. Many of the people coming for wheelchairs were from the southern part of Gaza, traveling with their children and the elderly. They were often turned away. The social workers we worked alongside were getting dozens of phone calls, letting them know the Israeli soldiers and settlers were not allowing them to come up. Unfortunately, we couldn't do anything about it. Because we wanted to deliver the wheelchairs to people who needed them, the social workers announced the opportunity on Palestinian radio, saying that anyone with a disability could show up and be given a wheelchair.

Palestine was often in the news at this time. There had been another intifada, the second Palestinian uprising against Israel. It resulted in many wounded people, and most people assumed that we were bringing chairs to the victims of the recent violence. The fact was that none of the chairs were given to that population. All of the chairs were given to those with disabilities. All of the recipients had been waiting for a wheelchair for a long time, including kids and the elderly.

About the third day of the seating clinic, early in the morning, the governor of Gaza City wanted the whole team to drop what we were doing and have tea with him in his office. We told him we couldn't do it during the day because of the number of patients. He kept sending people to repeat his invitation, and after the fifth time, we decided that four out of ten of our team members would leave the therapists and seating specialist and go to the office to have tea.

The governor was a member of the Fatah party, which was later voted out by the Hamas party for their corruption. Immediately after his staff served us, he received a phone call and was informed the Israelis were bulldozing down an olive orchard. It seemed to us this made his blood boil. He turned to us, hoping that we would share his indignation toward the Israelis. I told him, not wanting to take sides and not knowing the situation, that the Israelis needed to obey their prophets. In particular, Micah 6:8 instructs us, "He hath shewed thee, O man, what is good; and what doth the Lord require of thee, but to do justly, and to love mercy, and to walk humbly with thy God?" The governor immediately changed the subject. Just before leaving, he gave us gifts. I still have the large traditional ceramic bowl he gave me. I was asked about the bowl when I was leaving the country. I showed the official the governor's card, but they still sent it off for X-rays before we left.

The minister of health hosted a dinner in our honor, and we went to the ministry where we ate wonderful Middle Eastern food. However before dinner, they showed us a gory slideshow of wounded people from the battles, making us lose our appetites. I knew that wasn't their intent, but in their desire to show us their authentic struggles, they felt the need to show us the reality of their lives in the Gaza Strip. We hoped to return to Gaza in the near future, as the need was great.

Later in 1998, I drove a truck filled with wheelchairs to be shipped to Panama from southern Georgia for a ministry called Map International. A few days before I left, I called my friends, the Chenoweth's, who were living in Columbia, Missouri. Randy and Kathy had traveled in the Assembly with us in the early 1970s.

I was going to be passing through Columbia and hoped to see them. When they answered the phone, they expressed their amazement. Randy had just been in his backyard talking to a neighbor. His neighbor's name was Mel West, and Mel invited Randy to see the hand-crank, wheelchair cart he was building in his garage. Randy told him about Hope Haven International and my work there, hoping that he could introduce us "some day." To their delight, shortly after he met Mel, I called them to let them know I was coming. These were two amazing coincidences. Only God!

I drove the twelve-ton truck to the Chenoweth's house, parked it, and went over to meet Mel. As we walked together toward his garage, Mel told mehe used to be on the International Board for Habitat for Humanity. I asked him if he knew Bill Clark who also served on the board. Mel told me he did and that they were both on the Thousand Mile March together. Bill was the person who had procured the grant for us to start the wheelchair repair shop in Guatemala with Chito Pichya. Bill also invited me to get involved in the Rotary Clubs, which proved to be one of our greatest partners. This conversation gave Mel and me an immediate, great connection.

We went into Mel's garage and on his worktable was a crude, hand-crank, steel and wood cart. This cart became the ground floor of what was first called PET International, now Mobility Worldwide. We became their main distributors. I have been one of their consultants and on their medical advisory committee.

Ten years later in 2008, I was at my house in Guatemala when I received a call from the U.S. Navy. Paul Brown was the contractor who managed Project Handclasp. Project Handclasp is a humanitarian program of the United States Navy, which was started in 1962 to distribute materials and medical help. They help non-profits get relief goods to destinations on Navy ships, which are already going to those places. They tended to like wheelchairs and the hand-cranked chairs because they usually went through customs quickly.

We had shipped some chairs on their ships before, but they now had space available on a half dozen ships with immediate room for between two and three thousand wheelchairs, going to six different countries. Hope Haven was in the position to ship around 1,000 in this time frame.

I told Paul we wanted to go to Guatemala, Ecuador, Peru, Liberia, South America, and Central America, which were all on the ports of call for these cargo ships. I also told him I'd call PET to see if they had chairs ready to go. Like many of us, shipping was their biggest expense. When I first called Von Driggs, the operations director at PET, I couldn't get ahold of him. The PET office in Columbia, Missouri told me that Von was at a conference in Indiana and gave me the number of the family he was staying with. When I reached him with the news, I also mentioned I was leaving the following day for the States and had a long layover in Dallas, Texas but would call him again. Amazingly, he also had a layover in Dallas at the same time! Von got off the plane, we talked, and within a few months, PET had gotten over 1,200 PET wheelchairs shipped for free.

In November 1999, I co-found a loosely formed organization called the Association of Mobility Providers. With the help of an engineer named Hudson Moore, we contacted all of the people who were in the wheelchair and wheelchair delivery arenas. The wheelchair repair facility, now in Chimaltenango, Guatemala, after being moved from Momostenango in 1993, was still managed by Chito Pichya. Because of its central location, we decided to hold the conference there. We contacted the director of the Bible seminary, which was near the wheelchair repair shop and made arrangements to rent the facility during their summer break from November to January.

During the second week of November we held the conference and brought in different ministries, individuals, and organizations, which had been involved in delivering wheelchairs throughout the world. We had about twenty different organizations from ten different countries present. This was five years before USAID, the United States Agency for International Development, started facilitating their conferences. There had been some meetings in Africa, but as far as we knew, this was the first of its kind in Latin America. A lot of organizations were there, including Wheels for Humanity, Richard St. Denis (who later founded the World Access Project), the Mobility Project, Motivation (whose director also represented Whirlwind), Children's Medical Ministries, Telethon Honduras, DaVida (meaning "to give life") from Colombia, Wheelchair Sports International, Transitions, Bethel Ministries, Wheels of Hope, and representatives from wheelchair shops from El Salvador and Mexico. This first meeting was an opportunity for everyone to meet and communicate their goals and vision.

The following year in 2000, we had another meeting, representing many of the same groups as well as PET International. Out of these meetings important partnerships were formed, which to this day, are still in existence. These historical meetings brought a lot of the world's players together from the wheelchair delivery sector. Now, with better communication and technology, many of these groups find it easier to work together from afar.

In early 2000, the Safari Club Foundation contacted me because of one of its members, Kenneth E. Behring. Ken's wife, Pat, had heard of Wheels for the World and made a donation from her social security check each month to sponsor some wheelchairs. Ken and Pat were from Monroe, Wisconsin, and Ken had gone to the University of Wisconsin in Madison to play football. He was studying city planning but after one year, he left school and moved to Florida. In south Florida, he became one of the region's biggest developers. Later, he moved to Danville, California and developed one of the most exclusive housing developments in the state called Blackhawk. In the 1980s, he bought the Seattle Seahawks and owned them for about ten years, a very lucrative investment. He eventually sold them to Paul Allen, the cofounder of Microsoft.

Ken organized a small wheelchair project, flying some wheelchairs to Romania using the Safari Club as an umbrella. He then wanted to do something personally, and his representative from the Safari Club called me. I told him we would be doing a distribution in a month. I invited Ken to come with us to Hanoi and Hai Phong, Vietnam on this distribution voyage. I believed it would be important for him to come to experience giving away wheelchairs. Ken agreed and hired a film crew and a photographer to fly in and join him, and his representative from the Safari Club Foundation. They joined the Hope Haven team, which included a physical therapist, occupational therapist, rehabilitation technicians, and a rehabilitation engineer. The distribution trip was a powerful experience. Ken has told the story of the trip many times, and it can be found in his book, *The Road to Leadership: Finding a Life of Purpose.*

During this week in Vietnam, the experiences were life changing. The first wheelchair Ken gave away was to a girl about eight years old. A couple of days later, we were in Hai Phong, and they brought in an eighty-year-old woman. Through our translator, she thanked Ken for the wheelchair. She told him she had wanted to die but was now looking forward to living. In his book, he tells how this young girl and this elderly woman profoundly affected him. By then, Ken had already made up his mind that he was going to buy a lot of wheelchairs and help a lot of people in this way. He had already donated millions of dollars to the Smithsonian Institute. In fact, the rotunda at the National Museum of American History is named after the Behring family, who has also provided valuable contributions to the National Museum of Natural History.

When we flew back to the States, Ken and I stopped in Taiwan to visit the Heartway Wheelchair Factory. Heartway built Breezy 2 wheelchairs for Sunrise Medical, an innovative wheelchair manufacturer. My brother David arranged the meeting through the main purchaser in Asia for Sunrise Medical. After taking a tour of the factory, we were taken onto the showroom floor, which displayed all of the models of wheelchairs they built. We went through the different models, and I explained to the plant manager and president, as well as Ken, what features were best in a standard wheelchair for the developing world. We agreed on a sturdy frame, durable wheels and tires, swing-away footrests, detachable armrests, and nylon upholstery. We also decided on five different wheelchair widths. We went to their boardroom and sat at the big table, giving their plant manager some time to crunch numbers. Ken then signed a contract to purchase his first 10,000 wheelchairs.

Ken asked me when we'd have our next wheelchair delivery. We had one coming up in Guatemala and were working with First Lady Evelyn de Portillo. Within three weeks, I was in the presidential palace, meeting with Evelyn, to set up a wheelchair delivery. A month later, we were there with the wheelchairs. We all flew down in Ken's plane with a team of wheelchair experts, which I had handpicked. The plane, an MD-88 (DC 9), was originally configured to carry

125 passengers. Ken had converted it into a plane with a kitchen, twenty-two first-class seats, and his personal bedroom with a king-sized bed in the back. We had about forty chairs delivered to the Livermore airport near Danville, California. Ken had forty more standard wheelchairs sent via air-cargo from the Invacare factory in Mexico. It was a very successful wheelchair delivery where we gave away about half of the chairs in the presidential palace. The only reason the president wasn't there was that he was out of the country.

Evelyn was so impressed that she set up a meeting with all of the other Central American first ladies. Just over a year later, in October 2001, I was on another trip in Ken's plane. We filled the hull of the plane with wheelchairs and distributed them in Nicaragua, Honduras, and El Salvador with their first ladies. On our first stop in Nicaragua, Ken personally met the president. The rest of us worked with the vice-president, who had been part of the delivery. Within a month, the vice-president was elected president. I was a little uncomfortable that Enrique Bolanos had used this wheelchair delivery to gain votes.

While in Honduras doing the wheelchair delivery in the presidential palace, the first lady invited the president to come for a photo shoot. President Flores was so impressed that he stayed through the whole delivery. We finished off in El Salvador with the first lady delivering wheelchairs. Ken made it possible to create awareness with the first ladies and the presidents. To this day, the first ladies' offices seem to have more awareness and more social workers, attempting to identify the needs of the disabled. It's not perfect, but is a step in the right direction.

Ken had also invited three of the leaders of the LDS Charities (the humanitarian arm of The Church of Jesus Christ of Latter-day Saints) to come on his plane for this delivery. This inspired the Latter Day Saints to develop a wheelchair delivery and training program within their charities.

Ken Behring wanted to hire my brother David and me to help with his foundation. They would be delivering a one-size-fits-all model, which definitely has its place and is helpful. However, I chose to remain with Hope Haven International, doing the more complex rehabilitation and individualized wheelchairs.

Within twelve years, Ken's wheelchair foundation had celebrated giving away its one-millionth wheelchair. As a result of Ken wanting to help the disabled, there were different spin-off groups, including The Wheelchair Foundation of Canada, The Wheelchair Foundation of England, and the American Wheelchair Mission founded by Chris Lewis, the son of Jerry Lewis. Chris is following in his father's footsteps by helping people with disabilities. Chris' daughters are very active, too, following in their grandfather's footsteps.

CHAPTER 15

NURTURING THE SEEDLINGS

At least forty to fifty percent of the need for wheelchairs was for small children. We were still putting them in chairs that were too big. These chairs were hard to propel and made it difficult for the children to function.

Around 2000, four senior design students from the engineering department of Dordt College in Sioux Center, Iowa approached me. Dordt was about fifteen miles from Hope Haven's main shop, and we had caught their interest. They informed me that they needed a design project in order to graduate, suggesting they could provide ideas on a simple crutch or walker. I told them of our pediatric wheelchair challenge and my concern with welded wheelchairs. Welding was not only a hard skill to learn but could be very dangerous to welders' eyes and lungs. There was also the potential of the welder getting burned. We had just received a large donation from Sunrise Medical of old inventory from the KidCart factory they had acquired in Belgrade, Montana. Part of that donation was 5000 feet of ¾" powder coatee aluminum tubing which was coated light blue. The unique thing about the KidCart Pediatric Stroller was there were no welds in the design. Instead, they used plastic to couple the aluminum together. We loved their design, but it was primarily a stroller for just very young children.

About a year before this, I had been at the Rehabilitation Engineering Society of North America's annual conference in Long Beach, California where I gave a talk about Hope Haven International and refurbishing wheelchairs. Right after my presentation, Ralf Hotchkiss, who had just returned from Uganda, gave a slideshow, which documented him training a disabled women's group how to build the Whirlwind Wheelchair that he had designed years before in Nicaragua. Ralf has been the leader in sustainable wheelchair shops around the world. His presentation showed women welding. I decided, one way or another, I was going to design a wheelchair that made welding unnecessary. I sketched out ideas on a piece of paper, showing how to bend and couple tubes together with plastic blocks and let the students run with it. It wasn't long until they had a rough version of a workable concept.

Since then, we've worked with many universities for our design work, but more importantly, to have the students do both lab and field-testing. I've come to the conviction that testing is essential. Once we had a proven frame, we had to critique some of the dimensions to get it proportioned correctly. Then, the students proved how strong it was when it worked. We used recycled plastic from a local supplier. Next, we made a simple seat with limited growth potential and took the frame to Dr. Bob Jones in Wisconsin at Metalcraft Industries. Dr. Jones was a rehabilitation engineer who had run the University of Wisconsin's rehabilitation department some years earlier. He consulted and helped to develop the saddle bracket. Another consultant was Gib Fink, an occupational therapist who had spent his adult life in the wheelchair industry. He owned a company in the Chicago area called Therafin. Gib manufactured seating systems, and we worked together to produce the seating hardware. We also asked Larry and Cathy Mulholland of Mulholland Seating and Positioning for advice on the design. The Mulhollands are pioneers in growth systems for children.

All of these industry leaders helped us develop the Hope Haven KidChair into what it is today. Along with them, we've acquired a lot of feedback from other physical and occupational therapists, rehabilitation technicians, and perhaps most importantly, wheelchair users, parents, and caregivers. There's a saying among the wheelchair users of the developing world, which states "nothing about us without us."

Originally, the chairs were built using components in Ireton, Iowa, and the upholstery work done was in the South Dakota State Prison. The brackets were produced in the prison at Springfield, South Dakota. Later, volunteers did the carpentry work from the Apostolic Church in Rock Rapids, Iowa. In a twenty-year period, we had more than one million community service hours donated by inmates from three different prisons in South Dakota.

In May 2001, a school for children with disabilities in Kathmandu, Nepal contacted us with a wheelchair request. We were challenged by some partners there to bring wheelchairs in for the children. They were trying to work with a Rotary Club in England but never managed to get a matching grant. We were able to work with Ken Behring who sponsored the chairs. Other missionaries helped by providing the details and preparing for the distribution.

Our partners in Nepal didn't know how to do a wheelchair delivery and thought we could work out of a roadside storage room. We convinced them we needed a bigger facility and went to a nicer hotel, using the courtyard near the pool. On the second day of the distribution, a couple brought a Buddhist gentleman, now a Christian, who was a quadriplegic, laying flat in the back of a pickup truck. He had previously made a pilgrimage to India to see the Dalai Lama. While in India, he dove into a river and hit a rock, breaking his neck. Some loving Christians took him in and cared for him. We were able to get him in a reclining wheelchair with elevating leg rests so that he could be pushed around and have a more comfortable life.

We were able to worship with the local believers in Kathmandu. They met in secret since it was illegal to be a Christian. It was a blessing to be able to worship with them. We had to climb up four flights of steps and leave our shoes at the door. The men were on one side, and the women sat on the other side during worship. This reminded me of worshipping in the central highlands of Vietnam in a leper colony where they practiced the same tradition. This wasn't foreign to me as it's also how the Amish worship.

On the last day of our time there, we were able to take a fly-by in a tourist prop plane with large windows. The view of Mt. Everest and the Himalayas was amazing. Next to Machu Picchu in Peru, and perhaps Yellowstone in the winter, it was the most breathtaking experience of my life. Just before leaving, we decided to take a tour, so three of us hopped on motorcycles and drove around Kathmandu with one of the missionary's teenage sons. When we reached the bypass around the city, the police had stopped the traffic. The missionary's son said, "Someone important must be coming."

We waited and waited. About twenty minutes later, a Mercedes drove by and he said, "That's the queen." No sooner had they passed did he add, "And that's the king driving!"

This was a turbulent time in Nepal. About ten days after we were there, on June 1, the king and queen were killed by their own son. He was distraught because they did not approve of the girl he wanted to marry.

We have yet to go back to Nepal. It was our goal to go back and set up a wheelchair assembly or manufacturing plant there. We had found a local wheelchair manufacturing shop with a whole room of dusty wheelchairs. They were of poor quality with an even worse design. This plant had the problem that so many of these small shops have—they are able to get the initial funding to build and manufacture chairs, but their donors think they can set up a market and sell them. In reality, people who need wheelchairs cannot afford them. Even in the United States, were it not for third party payers, there would not be much of a wheelchair industry.

In June 2001, I brought Pastor Bil Vandyken, Hope Haven's religious services coordinator, to Guatemala. We had recently been approved for a grant from the Riverside Foundation, a foundation, which included Chuck Colson and Joni Eareckson Tada as board members. The year before, Joni had recommended we put in a proposal to do a wheelchair Bible camp in Romania. Unfortunately, because there was so much awareness for the plight of the disabled in Romania, a lot of other grants also came in for them and we did not get approved. Because Joni knew my heart for Guatemala, she encouraged us to do a similar proposal for Guatemala instead of Romania. We were approved for a $30,000 grant!

I took Pastor Bill down with me, and on this trip, we set up different meetings with various non-profits to bring partners together for a successful camp. We had meetings with the Central American Bible Seminary, Faith in Practice, Bethel Ministries, and Common Hope.

The Guatemalan schools' summer break starts in November and ends in late January. A three-week Bible camp was developed that included four days for children, four days for youth, and four days for adults. Bill did a great job developing an edifying Christian theme and curriculum for each year. He ended up leading the camps for the first twelve years. One of the things that Bill and I did on this trip was bring down one of the first Hope Haven KidChairs. He and I were able to personally give it away to a little girl in San Juan, Sacatepequez. The Bible camp thrived and Hope Haven later brought on partners from Hope Haven Canada in the Vancouver and British Columbia areas and Heritage Christian School in Rochester, New York.

Exactly a year after 9/11, in 2002, we were delivering wheelchairs in Ramallah, a Palestinian city on the central West Bank. Sandy and I were there with Greg Skolaski and Tom Glumac, both therapists.

Afterward, we spent the next few days in Bethlehem. While there, the Imam from the mosque across from the Church of the Nativity came by and saw what we were doing. Just a month before, the Israelis had been in Bethlehem. The city had a curfew, and people could only leave their houses once every four days to get food and water. When we went in the church, we saw countless bullet holes and much damage. This was during Ramadan and the Muslims were fasting, but the Imam from the mosque gave us a tour and invited us to his house so that we could share their meal, which they couldn't eat until after sunset. He had two daughters, about ten and twelve years old. Sandy gave the girls gifts, and the older girl received a jump rope. She just lit up and told us that it was her birthday. This was just another example of Palestinian hospitality. This is something you never forget, especially in light of all of the hatred so many Christians now have towards the Palestinians.

In October 2003, we did another wheelchair delivery with 200 wheelchairs to be shipped to the West Bank. They were delivered to Ramallah, Jenin, and Tulkarm. The chairs were shipped in plenty of time, and when we knew they had cleared customs, we bought our tickets. Our team came in and we spent the first few days in east Jerusalem on the Mount of Olives. We were waiting on word that the wheelchairs could get out of the port, but there was a strike by the dockworkers. The container was stuck. Rather than sitting around and feeling sorry for ourselves, we spoke to the host and asked to survey some sites and hospitals in order to evaluate needs.

Our visits in Bethlehem, Hebron, and east Jerusalem were eye-opening, making the desperate need clear. One evening we asked a few of the others if they wanted to go and visit some of our old friends. In 1991 and 1992, when I was the shipping manager at Phil's Greenhouse, I had met Israel and Pnina Comforti. Pnina was an expert in tissue culture and had been brought to Ohio to work in a joint project with Phil's Greenhouse and the kibbutz. Israel was a truck driver and had worked with me in shipping. We had become very good friends. In less than two years, they had moved back to Israel. The whole family had become Christians, and they became pillars in the Messianic church in Israel.

We decided to go and visit them and walked down the Mount of Olives. We jumped on a bus and went to Ashdod where Pnina's son Koby picked us up. From there, we went to Pnina's pie shop in nearby Gan Yavne. Pnina was actually a renowned pastry chef who had made the national news. Just because she was a Messianic Jew, some of the stricter rabbis wanted to disqualify her restaurant as being un-kosher. The lawsuit went all the way to the highest courts, but the Comfortis won the suit and Pnina was able to share her faith on national television.

While we were there, her oldest son Koby had just finished his four-year stint in the Israeli Defense Force (IDF). I hadn't seen him since 1999. We explained to Koby what we were doing with the wheelchairs. As soon as they got out of port, we were going to do a distribution in Nablus. He told us he had spent his entire four years in the IDF being trained for and assigned to Nablus.

Nablus is an interesting place. It's in the old Biblical Samaria, where Jesus met the woman at the well. Jews were not to associate at all with Samaritans, but Jesus ignored the law and offered the woman compassion and love (John 4). In current times, Jews treat Palestinians in the same way they treated the Samaritans 2000 years ago. When we arrived in Nablus two nights later, the volunteers that were organizing the patients briefed us on the situation. They told us that they would be back in the morning to take us to the site where the wheelchair delivery would take place. After taking a tour of the historic old city of Nablus, we went back at the hotel. Early the next morning, during breakfast, our hosts came in and they all looked like they hadn't slept a wink. They asked us if we were okay, and we responded that we were well rested. They told us that throughout the night, there had been street fighting and gunfire between the Israeli soldiers and the Palestinians. Fortunately, each of our rooms had its own air conditioning unit, which sounded like jet engines so none of our team had heard the gunfire. Blessings!

We went to the warehouse, which was just an old building rented by the UN. We arrived early and waited for the forty-foot sea container to arrive. Slowly, patients started to arrive. We anxiously waited, hoping the wheelchairs would arrive at any moment. It wasn't long before our host answered a call from the truck driver. The Israelis would not allow him to come into Nablus.

Steve Sosebee, myself, and three others grabbed a taxicab and went straight to the border crossing, less than two miles away. We confronted the soldiers who were standing in front of the truck. They basically told us to get out of there and told the truck driver they'd let him in the next day. This was the day before the Sabbath, and we figured they'd use that as an excuse the next day to not let him in again.

Upon arriving in Israel at the Ben-Gurion airport, I had rented a cell phone and had only managed to enter one phone number, Israel and Pnina's home number. I knew that Israel wasn't there because he was off working in the southern part of Israel, but he was a captain in the IDF reserves. I dialed the number and Koby answered the phone.

"Koby, we're at the checkpoint, and they won't let the wheelchairs in."

He wanted to know which one of the two crossings we were dealing with and asked to talk to the officer in charge. So I turned to the soldier who had told us to leave and asked him whom the officer in charge was. He gave me a dirty look, but not knowing whom I had on the phone, he had to comply and pointed me to a secure area, surrounded by sandbags. I walked over there and again asked for the commanding officer. The officer identified himself and I handed him the phone.

Within thirty seconds, he handed the phone back and told the soldiers to let the truck through. They knew Koby was an officer who had served there. This was yet more evidence of God's divine intervention. Without our connection with Koby and our ability to contact him since he was out of the IDF, who knows if or when we would have gotten the wheelchairs. We spent that day distributing wheelchairs in Nablus. We put the remaining wheelchairs in old UN trucks and separated to do seating clinics in Jenin and Tulkarm.

Years later, possibly June 2010, we were living in Guatemala and sent Ben to work with Wheelchair Angels and do a wheelchair delivery in Nablus. Nablus was an amazing place for Ben to be. What better place to teach your sixteen-year old the principal of being a Good Samaritan than in the place where Samaria had been, where Jesus had shown so much compassion and love for a woman his culture would have despised. I'm glad Ben followed in my footsteps . . . as far as his love of travel and his compassion for the poor.

CHAPTER 16

SOME SOW, OTHERS REAP

The fall of 2004 was a terrible hurricane season for Florida. Four hurricanes hit the state—Charley, Frances, Ivan, and Jeanne.

In the early summer, we had shipped wheelchairs to Peru in collaboration with ROC Wheels. For some reason, we assumed we'd ship them and in thirty to forty days, they would be there. After fifty days, we were looking at getting tickets to send the whole distribution team. We checked to make sure everything was in place and realized the chairs weren't there. The shipping company had never bothered to tell us that the wheelchairs, which were sent to New York, had not been put on ships because of the hurricanes. A month later, they put them on a ship but were offloaded in a Caribbean port because of the hurricanes in the Caribbean. A week later, again, they told us they couldn't load them because the crane broke. After all these delays, they were finally on their way.

We arrived in Peru, but after three days, we grew tired of waiting for the wheelchairs. A couple of us went from Lima to Guayaquil in Ecuador to see if we could get some wheelchairs from a partner who was working there. We took a bus to Santo Domingo de los Colorados and managed to salvage another distribution. This group was a non-profit called Vista Para Todos, which means, "sight for all." They, too, were waiting on wheelchairs as theirs were stuck in customs. We had a lot of experience with that, so we helped them get their chairs out. This, in itself, turned the delay into a blessing. Our team in Peru switched plans and went to Machu Picchu first instead of after the distribution as planned. By the time we returned, the wheelchairs were there, and the trip had transformed into a good one.

This trip to Ecuador was the first time I saw tribal people with cell phones. They still performed traditional dancing, engaged in body painting, played bamboo flutes, and maintained other traditions, but it was disconcerting to see them using the phones.

New opportunities opened up for us. United Airlines had stopped flying to Vietnam with the fall of Saigon in 1975. After nearly thirty years, in 2004, their first flight back into Vietnam had a load of thirty-six wheelchairs on it. The VIPs on board were American actor David Hasselhoff, his wife Pamela, and Team Quickie, an entire wheelchair basketball team. The year before, David Hasselhoff had gone with my brother, David, to Costa Rica to distribute wheelchairs.

In 2005, we headed to Uzbekistan. When we arrived, we were told that our three containers with the wheelchairs had been cleared in customs, but they were still in port and wouldn't get final release until another official signed the papers. We only had one week to deliver 600 chairs to seven parts of the country. The first day was spent going to the railroad station. Uzbekistan is one of the few double-landlocked countries in the world. They not only have no seaport, but you have to go through two other countries to get there. As we waited, the company decided they wanted their containers back, so they cross stuffed the chairs into eight smaller containers. It took a while, but we got to the port and within three hours, they started to deliver the smaller containers to a government nursing home that Samaritan's Purse was using as a distribution site. While part of the team was delivering wheelchairs, the other part was taking the rest out and loading them into six different trucks to go to the other six locations. Each location had about sixty people waiting for them. We broke them down and sent, to the best of our knowledge, the appropriate wheelchairs for each destination.

After we stayed for two days in Tashkent, the capital of Uzbekistan, to do a distribution, we broke up into two teams.

One story stood out for me at the Tashkent Senior Center. There was a mother who had two daughters that were about six years old, both needing a wheelchair. The mother could only carry one child at a time, so she couldn't take the girls to school. With the Hope Haven KidChairs that she received, she could now take the kids to school. She was so excited and so grateful for this blessing.

I went with one team to the Ferghana Valley, east of Tashkent, and Mark Hawkins and Sara Risser took the other team to deliver in the southwestern part of the country. Andijan was the first city we visited. There was a WWII veteran who came for a wheelchair, wearing a jacket with all of his medals on it.

On Easter Sunday, Samaritan's Purse and our wheelchair distribution team woke up in Namangan, Uzbekistan. We had just completed the week of distributions. Altogether, we had distributed the nearly 600 wheelchairs in seven different cities.

We had a five-hour drive to get back to the capital city, Tashkent, in time for the afternoon Easter Sunday church services. After we returned to the guesthouse in Tashkent, some went to worship with the Uzbek believers at an Uzbek church, while I joined the not-so-adventurous ones attending the English Fellowship Church. By the time we arrived, the sanctuary was full. We stood in the back expecting to enjoy the service standing room only. However, an usher came and took me to the second row and found a space for me right next to a Korean couple. The children from the church, all belonging to the English-speaking families, performed their Easter play. What a blessing it was to see these children, coming together from many parts of the English-speaking world, perform the resurrection story in this largely Muslim country.

After the service, I introduced myself to the Korean couple. It turned out that Ronald Hong was an orthotist, as well as the president of the New Hope Rehabilitation Foundation in Tashkent. He invited me to come and see the center at some point in the future. When he learned we were returning to the States early the next morning, he took us right after the service. We both knew it was no accident that we were seated in the same pew that Easter afternoon.

Halfway into touring the center, I realized we had tons of rehabilitation orthopedic supplies, wheelchairs, and PETs (Personal Energy Transports) sitting in a warehouse back in South Dakota, which they could use. We also had boxes of shoes and sweaters that had come in, just waiting for a place to be shipped. He had been praying for all these things.

It was amazing how, over the next few months, one thing after another fell into place. We were able to load not just one, but two forty-foot sea containers for the New Hope Rehabilitation Center. Only through God's divine intervention and our obedience could we have become, for them, the hands and feet of Jesus.

Because Uzbekistan is a double-landlocked country, it takes sea containers twice as long to arrive. I gave thanks when I received an email from Uzbekistan, reporting that they had completed the distribution of all of the supplies we'd sent. I was glad to hear that most of the items were distributed in the Ferghana Valley in eastern Uzbekistan.

On the drive from Namangan to Tashkent, that Easter morning, we had driven over the mountain pass on The Silk Road. The Silk Road was an ancient network of trade routes, which linked countries for the purpose of commerce. We came across a scene I will never forget. There were at least one hundred sheep walking on the side of the road as we passed. I asked the driver of the van to let me out to get a better picture. I snapped a few photos of the shepherd on horseback holding a sick sheep—a black one at that! I was reminded of Luke 15:4 when Jesus had asked, "…who wouldn't leave the ninety nine to find the one lost sheep?"

Unfortunately, many of the missionaries we met while in Uzbekistan were unable to get visas to stay to continue their work. Most people in Uzbek's population are Sunni Muslims. When I was in Onnenjon, the one thing that really stood out to me was that after we would give a wheelchair, especially to the elderly, they would start praying. After a few did that, I asked the translators what they were doing and found out that they were praying for me! The Muslims were praying that they would see us in paradise. This broke the stereotype so many believe that all Muslims believe Christians are going to hell. The people were so thankful, and I was just so amazed that they would be praying for us.

They knew that we were Christians. The Muslims understood the value of giving the wheelchairs to the poor who needed them.

Another interesting and beautiful tradition was that before we shook their hands, the Muslims would hold their hand over their heart as a sign of respect. When they prayed, they would pray with their hands stretched out. I also had an interesting situation with a husband and wife. He was disabled and his wife was always near him. He had only a few teeth left, all plated with silver. Interesting enough, she had most of her teeth, and they were all plated with gold. I wasn't sure what to make of that! My experience with the Muslims has always been that they are so kind.

In August 2005, Hurricane Katrina struck Louisiana. Samaritan's Purse contacted us immediately. We helped by using our buying power and getting many wheelchairs to Shreveport. Hope Haven had a booth at LifeLight, a large outdoor Christian music festival in Sioux Falls, South Dakota, and I was there displaying our KidChair. Samaritan's Purse told me that they knew the eye of the storm was hitting land and a lot of elderly people were being evacuated and taken to Shreveport. They were in such a rush that the rescue workers had to leave behind their mobility equipment, including wheelchairs, walkers, and canes. I knew of a large wheelchair company that was donating all of their offshore returns because they had no system to repackage the equipment. It was actually cheaper for them to throw or give them away. When the hurricane hit, we called this company. We signed a contract, which said we wouldn't give away anything in the United States, and they gave us an exemption and a truck full of mobility equipment to send down to Louisiana.

Another company we had been getting wheelchair parts from had 500 standard wheelchairs available, sitting in a warehouse. We purchased them on credit and had them delivered to Samaritan's Purse within a few days. This was a good example of two non-profits and two companies in the industry working together and getting over 700 wheelchairs and hundreds of crutches, walkers, and canes to where they were needed. In normal circumstances, this would have taken weeks, but because of the networking and cooperation, it was accomplished in a few days.

In 2007, in partnership with Samaritan's Purse and Sara Riser, we shipped a container of wheelchairs to Ecuador to be delivered primarily in San Miguel Bolivar and at the Christian school in Quito. We flew into Quito and, on our way to San Miguel, we traveled through the Avenue of the Volcanoes and were able to take pictures with some of the lama shepherds. This was at the base of Chimborazo, one of the impressive volcanoes. We were in awe of the breathtaking views, feeling like we'd gone back in time. These folks still live what most would consider a very primitive lifestyle, much like their Inca ancestors. They were kind enough to let us take pictures with them and their lamas.

We were given a few hundred shoes from Lands End in Dodgeville, Wisconsin and stopped at an orphanage to give the shoes to the kids. This was a wonderful, heartwarming experience as the team played out on the lawn and playground with the kids. Most of our team was from Living Springs Church in Brandon, South Dakota, and Torrey and Heather Babb had joined us on their second wheelchair delivery.

Torrey and Heather have hearts for the Lord and for youth ministry. During this trip, the concept for a ministry called the Mission Ball was birthed. While in San Miguel, we witnessed a bunch of young boys kicking around a soccer ball that was made up of plastic bags wrapped together. Torrey went and bought a couple of soccer balls, and in the early evening, the team started playing soccer with the kids. The kids were thrilled to get to play with real soccer balls!

One year later, Torrey came to Guatemala while we were setting up the Hope Haven Guatemala wheelchair factory. He made contacts with a company that was having some of their soccer balls sewn in the Pavon prison. Probably prisoners sewed the first couple of hundred Mission Balls. He had worked with the company to print the gospel message and The Ten Commandments on the ball. Today, the Mission Ball is in forty different languages and has become a major tool for youth ministry and evangelism.

I was impressed that we were getting to go to this un-served area of San Miguel because of the history of the area. I learned that it was settled by some of the 16th-century persecuted Jews during the Peruvian Inquisition. It turned out to be a very unique community, and it had a police academy. The cadets came to help us with the delivery, carrying in the patients and helping families. We were very impressed with this class of future police officers.

Sara Risser had come to Ecuador over fifty years before with HCJB. HCJB was known as "The Voice of the Andes." It was the first radio station with daily programming in Ecuador and one of the first Christian missionary radio stations in the world. Because Ecuador was so high in elevation, the signal could go out all over the world. Sara, who was a nurse, worked in Hospital Vozandes for twenty years, starting a community development program before leaving the mission. She eventually left HCJB in 1983 and started many programs in Ecuador, including a foundation which provided health care opportunities, construction projects for churches to have compassion programs, and she worked with a development program that included a water program for digging and building wells.

In 1999, Sara had a youth group bring a wheelchair as a piece of luggage while working with a Rotary Club in Cuenca. This was a great time and a tool for sharing Jesus with those needing a wheelchair as well as their family members. Another one of her wheelchair deliveries used the U.S. Air Force to deliver wheelchairs to Ecuador. This was when I met her, in January of 2001, and helped her with her team to complete the wheelchair delivery in Cuenca and Quito, Ecuador. Sara later joined Hope Haven International in wheelchair deliveries in Nepal, Uzbekistan, Mexico, Colombia, Eritrea, and Peru, as well as many deliveries all over Ecuador. She has always been a joy to work with. For all who work with her, they can see she is filled with a desire to serve the Lord. Her sense of humor and dedication has been such an inspiration to me.

Samaritan's Purse, at this time, was raising lots of money through their Christmas catalog, which included wheelchairs to help kids with disabilities. They not only sponsored wheelchairs, but this enabled us to bring in the physical therapists and rehabilitation technicians to do the seating clinics. While we were in Ecuador, they sent some of their volunteers who had been doing disaster relief at a volcano eruption on the Peruvian border. These volunteers helped in many ways, but most importantly in praying with the recipients and their families in their native language. One of the members of our team commented on just how beautiful it was to watch the Samaritan's Purse volunteers, as well as Sara, praying and praising God with the recipients, usually with tears and embraces. It was such a beautiful testimony to the Godly desires of all involved while serving each other. "...but the Lord thy God turned the curse into a blessing unto thee, because the Lord thy God loved thee." (Deuteronomy 23:5b)

Our friends back in the United States were also busy. In 2007, Nick Mascitelli, a former district governor of Rotary International in northern California, had put together a Rotary matching grant with the Honduras Rotary Club, Real de Mines, in Tegucigalpa. The grant enabled them to sponsor a sea container of about 200 wheelchairs. This was the first of many future matching grants that Hope Haven International received by partnering with the Rotary International Foundation. These grants have helped thousands of people all over the world.

One family in Tegucigalpa had a particularly tragic story. They owned a little shop where they sold staples, such as napkins, toilet paper, and other personal hygiene products. At the end of one day when the husband was shutting the store down, some thieves came and shot him, leaving him paralyzed. His wife was pregnant at the time and gave birth to a baby. Between caring for both her husband, now a paraplegic, and the baby, they had to sell their entire inventory and shut down the shop. It seemed like the only way out of their dilemma was for her to leave him and the baby and illegally go to the United States to find a job so she could send money back. She left and they didn't hear anything for a few months. They finally got word from the police in Arizona that her body was found in the desert. She had starved to death. They think she became sick and the Coyotes, men who illegally bring people in, just left her to die. It was their Mother's Day when they got word she had died. Her husband wanted to continue to sell things. We gave him a PET wheelchair, and he could carry things in the trunk of the hand crank. We made an exception and gave him both a wheelchair and a PET to help him provide an income. "For I desired mercy, and not sacrifice; and the knowledge of God more than burnt offerings." (Hosea 6:6)

Just over the canyon from my house is a village called Santo Domingo Xenacoj. This village had been extremely isolated, with only dirt roads approaching it until the early 2000s. Xenacoj is unique in that it has its own dialect. Wycliffe had sent translators who were able to translate the New Testament into their dialect. Eventually, the churches' leadership teams received Bibles. A pastor visiting from Living Springs Church in Brandon, South Dakota, Kendall Carlson, challenged the churches and Wycliffe to provide a New Testament to every home in the community, rather than just leaving the Bibles at the Wycliffe site waiting to be purchased. I was able to raise money to get the Bibles out to the community. Back home in Ohio, the Alliance Christian Center accepted the challenge and sent funds. On one amazing Sunday, church leadership members and Christians from other communities in Guatemala met and divided into teams. Each team was given a section of town. Fifteen hundred homes received a New Testament in their native dialect that day. An unpredicted result was that the churches learned to work together. All of a sudden, there was a lot of revival happening, and it was a consolidated effort, almost like a crusade.

CHAPTER 17

RAIN AND SUNSHINE

n 2008, I had a strong feeling we should move back to Guatemala. At the same time, I knew that we needed to set up a successful pilot project of empowering wheelchair users to control their own lives by building their own wheelchairs and wheelchairs for others, as well as by being involved in the seating, manufacturing, and delivery of the wheelchairs.

I went into the office of David Vanningan, Executive Director of Hope Haven. I told him I was going to move back to Guatemala and set up manufacturing of the KidChair, with or without Hope Haven. I was stepping off a cliff, but I felt so strongly that this was our next step in this journey. In this way, we were also trying to meet the increasing needs for more wheelchairs. Because of the limited number of donated chairs available in the United States and Canada, we were never able to meet the huge need that existed.

I'd prepared myself, expecting David to say, "No thanks, nice knowing you." Instead, he said he was open to it but concerned as to how to fund the project. I had some ideas. First, I showed him a Rotary matching grant that we were working on for tools, parts, and completed KidChairs. It would be worth over $68,000. In addition, thanks to a contact my brother David had made, we had an order for 1,000 wheelchairs from the Mexicana Airline Foundation to be built and sent to Mexico City for the children at the Telethon Centers. We also had some support from donors—old friends living in Florida and California. We acquired a used van, which was donated from United Cerebral Palsy in Los Angeles, to drive down. We had found a 3,000-square-foot warehouse on the edge of Antigua, which we rented in March.

These ideas and donations were enough, and we received a commitment from Hope Haven. This was another important lesson for my whole family, one in which we truly follow where we sense God is leading. In response to our obedience, He provided the way.

So we sent Michael in April, and he started training wheelchair users to set up the shop and assemble wheelchairs. We sent a container-full of donated chairs and parts for the first one hundred Hope Haven KidChairs down, along with some volunteers from the Alliance Christian Center to help get the shop set up. Kurt Klingelhoffer, our friend who had built the rack on our GMC school bus eighteen years before, led the team. They built a mezzanine and office in the warehouse, which we had rented from a local factory that built high-end mahogany furniture.

Back in Brandon, South Dakota, we had the challenge of selling our house. This was right before the bottom fell out of the housing market, and I was already concerned that we weren't putting the house on the market quickly enough. Sandy wanted to get the house in perfect shape to sell, which took time. I kept worrying, but she reassured me, saying she just knew it'd be fine and to have faith and not worry.

Praise the Lord, not only did we sell and close on the house at the exact right moment, but we received full asking price. On the day, we finalized the sale of the house, closed on it at noon, jumped in the van, and Sandy, Ben, Matt, and I started driving to Guatemala. In Houston, we dropped Ben and Sandy off at the airport with our pet three-foot ball python and Sonic, the Pomeranian dog. Ben had the python, Obadiah, in a basket and just carried it in with him. I figured that if the airport refused to allow our python on, the snake would have to drive down with Matt and me, but he cruised through security with no questions asked. Some might consider this a miracle in itself!

Initially, we delivered about fifty completed wheelchairs at a time. We drove them roughly twenty-five miles to the Guatemala City airport and, through the Mexicana Foundation, they were shipped to Mexico City for free in cooperation with AeroMexico. The chairs were then given to children in Mexico City. We also held regular seating clinics in the facility.

Right around the time we moved to Guatemala, our pastor, Kendall Carlson at Living Springs Church in Brandon, noticed that the church was very scattered in terms of mission focus and felt it would be healthy for them to adopt a project. In this case, they wanted to adopt a whole town.

In July 2008, within ten days of us moving to Guatemala, Kendall came down. I had a few towns in mind, but I couldn't get Xenacoj out of my heart. So we went to Xenacoj and walked right into the mayor's office. Kendall was very critical of missionaries just coming in and shoving programs down the throats of the poor. He wanted to come and meet with the mayor and ask him what was most needed. We met for about a half-hour and the mayor, who was very open and welcoming, shared some ideas. When we walked out, one of the city policemen told us we needed to meet Filipa Chile, the founder and director of Guatemaltecas de Corazon.

We went and spoke with her in her office just two blocks away. We were very impressed with the community development programs she had for the children and elderly. Kendall's next step was to organize and invite all thirteen pastors in Xenacoj to a meeting to ask them what they thought was most needed. One of the main things they mentioned was leadership training for upcoming church leaders.

Four months later, Kendall and another team from Living Springs came down over Thanksgiving. One of Filipa's primary programs was providing a daily, hot meal program for the elderly—mainly women—who had been widowed during the war years before. One of the team members was Ray, who was a federal meat inspector. Guatemaltecas de Corazon had a large convection oven, which they used to teach baking to the women. The team decided to do a traditional American Thanksgiving with turkey, cornbread, cranberry sauce, and all of the traditional fixings. The Grandmas, our nickname for the widows, absolutely loved the meal but felt the need to add tortillas to the menu - a food item that is a part of every meal for them! The highlight for me was sharing the Thanksgiving story with them. They were fascinated by how the Native Americans saved the Pilgrims from starvation.

This was a good time for our three sons to become even more active in wheelchair ministry than they had been in the States. Michael helped to do the initial training for our workers in Guatemala, and through a USAID grant, he went with Wheels for Humanity to Yogyakarta, Indonesia to train them in the assembly of the Hope Haven KidChair. Matt worked part-time in the shop and spent half of his time in Spanish classes. Ben volunteered in the shop and helped with seating in Guadalajara, Oaxaca, Mexico and in the West Bank. He also made the Guatemala Jr. National basketball team when he was fifteen years old. It didn't hurt that he was the tallest of all of the athletes in the "14–17" age group in all of Central America. He was 6'7".

It wasn't long before we started to use faculty-led programs from American universities including the University of South Dakota, Emory University, the University of Mary in North Dakota, and Sacred Heart University in Connecticut. Later, the University of Missouri joined us. We worked with their physical therapy and occupational therapy programs, inviting the professors to bring their students down to Guatemala. These students worked side-by-side with the therapy students from Universidad Rafael Landívar. We've also worked with other universities, including the University of New Mexico and LeTourneau University in Longview, Texas. For the universities, it was an opportunity for students to get hands-on experiences, sometimes difficult in the United States because of liability issues.

In October 2000, God called Neil and Pam Donoghue to the mission field from Windborn Church, through the message of a visiting pastor from Chad, Africa. Neil, an operating engineer with Local 3, and Pam, a homeschooling mother of three, started preparing to leave their five-acre ranch and union life behind. They joined the mission organization WEC International, and in October 2002, they left for Chad. Because there was such a need for water in sub-Sahara, they were expecting to drill water wells.

When they arrived in Abeche, Chad, Neil began teaching welding skills to Muslim men who had left Islam and found Jesus as their Lord and Savior. In doing so, these men discovered they were left without a way to provide for their families. On his way to their small welding shop, Neil saw men and women crawling on the road—not just a few but many. One day, he asked their field leader, Dr. Louis Sutton, if there was a need for wheelchairs in Abeche. This is how their wheelchair ministry, Wheelchairs for the Least of These, began. Neil started researching a tricycle type of chair and built the first sixty chairs, one at a time, using the resources available in Abeche, according to the recipients' size and need.

One day while Neil was working on their kerosene refrigerator, their thirteen-year-old daughter, Megan, ran outdoors and into their kitchen with their flip phone saying, "Daddy, there's someone from America on the phone for you!"

I was calling from Hope Haven International. This was the first call that had come into them from outside Chad. I used Skype with credit to call their regular phone. I had been a friend of Katherine Clemons since we were both in our late teens, and Katherine went to church with the Donoghue family. She contacted me to let me know about the work Neil was doing, hoping I could offer some help. We offered a container of 180 wheelchairs. I told them about my relationship with PET International, and we were able to arrange their receipt of a container of PET wheelchairs. Even though these chairs were heavy and slow, they were the ideal mobility solution for that part of Africa.

When I first worked with PET in the late '90s, they were using wheelbarrow tires, which had inner tubes that constantly went flat. My brother David had put me in touch with Bill Knooihuizen from KIK Tire. Bill had developed a solid urethane tire for wheelbarrows and wheelchairs that wouldn't go flat, using nylon cords to keep them from coming off the rim. This turned out to be an amazing improvement, especially in northern Africa where the thorns of the acacia trees could puncture a truck tire.

These chairs could each be assembled in about forty-five minutes, as opposed to Neil's current timeframe of one chair a week. The Donahues prayed to see what doors the Lord would open to get the chairs to them. Miraculously, the Lord opened all of them! They developed a relationship with the UNHCR (United

Nations High Commissioner for Refugees) who then classified the shipment of this container with 180 wheelchairs as humanitarian, making the Donoghue family responsible for no taxes. In addition, the UNHCR made a deal with them that if Neil and his crew went into the Darfur refugee camps and did the distributions, the UN would give them another 200 chairs to distribute to the Chadian population. They were able to take their Christian welding students into the camps to help with distributions, and these students were able to tell the refugees that people who love Jesus had sent these chairs to help them. These chairs were a tangible expression of the love of Jesus to every single person who received or even saw them.

In all, 460 Chadians and Darfur refugees received the gift of mobility in the name of Jesus. When the Donoghue family left Chad in 2010, they left with hearts full of gratitude. The Donoghues now work out of California, leading their ministry Wheelchairs for the Least of These.

In 2011, Living Springs, my church from Brandon, South Dakota, again sent a team down. The goals for this trip included providing school supplies to the children in the village and building houses. The team also visited a house they had built the last time they were there in order to construct an outhouse to provide some privacy. Often, the sanitation for the very poor is not much more than a hole in the ground with some corn stalks tied together for privacy.

For one of the team members, a specific incident really stood out to her. As soon as the team arrived, she wanted to leave. For some reason, the area just felt evil to her, even though she really couldn't explain what she was feeling. The mother of the family came over and was very distraught. Her young daughter had tried to throw herself off a cliff twice in the past few days. She believed a demon was telling her to do it. The mother had asked for one of the pastors of the village to come and pray over her in order to combat this evil influence. Her fear was real and her daughter was quite scared. This incident truly brought to mind just how close people in dire poverty live to the spirit world.

In the United States, the little girl would have been brought to a hospital and most likely been diagnosed with a mental health condition. In this tiny, isolated village the people had always lived in tune with what was influencing them. Our team prayed for them, feeling such a sense of evil, yet power came in the Word.

"And he said unto them, Go ye into all the world, and preach the gospel to every creature. He that believeth and is baptized shall be saved; but he that believeth not shall be damned." (Mark 16: 15–16)

The living conditions for so many in this tiny village were very primitive. Often the people who visit want to "fix" what they assume are the problems. As an example, in the mid-70s, an Old Order Mennonite, Mervin Stauffer, went to southern Belize and began working in the San Jose, Toledo district in a Mopan-Mayan village. In this village, houses were made of split logs tied together with vines and thatched roofs with no indoor plumbing, so people just defecated on the jungle floor. Mervin got some concrete slabs, made wooden boxes with a hole in the top of them and put walls around them, creating outhouses. He made sure there were outhouses all over the village so they would no longer have to use the jungle floor. He came back the following winter to find out that none of the outhouses had been used. After investigating, he learned that people continued to go to the bathroom on the ground so that the dogs and pigs had something to eat. In this area, dogs were very valuable, warning the villages if outsiders were coming. The pigs were considered extremely valuable because they would eat the poisonous snakes. One animal protected them from unseen danger and the other from visible danger. This was a good example of what often happens when well-meaning people want to help but don't take into consideration the far-reaching ramifications of what they think is helpful. Besides, it's not that easy to change generational habits and systems. It doesn't matter how good an idea it is if the locals won't use it.

Many travel teams are shocked by the level of poverty they experience. At the same time, they're amazed by the joy and peace they see in so many of the villagers. It's often provided an amazing time of self-reflection for so many of our servants. "For our light affliction, which is but for a moment, worketh for us a far more exceeding and eternal weight of glory..." (2 Corinthians 4:17)

CHAPTER 18

STORMS

I n January 2010, I was in the Dominican Republic doing a wheelchair delivery at the Dominican Rehabilitation Association (DRA). The DRA was the same organization that Hope Haven had been helping prior to my coming to work for them. They had a sheltered workshop, providing employment to persons with developmental and physical disabilities. They were experiencing numerous power outages daily, a problem prevalent in the Dominican Republic (DR). There was a joke in the DR at that time: "*Donde hay sol y no hay luz?*" which means, "where there is sun, and there is no light?" So Hope Haven donated the funds to buy a generator.

About the third day into the wheelchair delivery, a small group of us were in downtown Santa Domingo eating at a restaurant when the ground below us started to roll and shake. I had a very uncomfortable feeling. I knew it was a severe earthquake but also thought it was very far away. I had felt the same motion a year before when an earthquake off the coast of Honduras had affected the Caribbean coast of Guatemala. This motion felt exactly the same.

I knew it had to be bad. After eating, we headed back to the hotel, and the first thing I did was get online. At that point, all I could find was general information about an earthquake on the Haiti side of the island, but soon the TV stations started talking about it constantly. This was the same earthquake we now know devastated Haiti. Haiti is a country in which we've been actively involved for a long time. We have sent over 640 wheelchairs to Haiti over the years.

In May 2010, a partnering organization, Familias De Esperanza, hosted a disaster response conference and made it available to all of the non-profits in Guatemala. We sent eight of our workers, mainly wheelchair users, to the conference where they learned how to respond to a natural disaster. It wasn't a week or two later when Agatha, the first tropical storm of the season, hit Guatemala and dropped twelve inches of rain in twenty-four hours. Every province in Guatemala was affected. Being a mountainous country, the people often live near rivers and streams. The water rose and many homes were flooded. In addition, there were landslides, including some resulting in whole buses being buried under the mud, killing everyone in them. Within three miles of our factory was the base of the volcano, Agua, and the landslides and mud from that area flowed into Ciudad Vieja and other nearby villages, filling up the houses with muddy water, sometimes up to six feet deep. Many people perished throughout Guatemala and some just a few miles from our factory.

The following day, we received a call from Tamalyn, the country director of Familias de Esperanza, asking us to find as many volunteers with shovels that we could. Her sister was there, organizing volunteers from churches for the disaster response. So I grabbed Ben and all the shovels we could find and drove to the contact point to find out where they would send us. When we arrived, we heard the strategy was to dig out the mud that was in the houses and bring it up to the road. Later, the skid loaders and trucks would come to haul it away. We realized that carrying a shovel load of mud from fifty to one hundred feet, just to throw it on the road, was not the most efficient plan. We decided that wheelbarrows or a bucket brigade was the way to go. There were many people willing to help but few shovels.

At HHI, we had been using three- and five-gallon buckets for parts' storage from a local hardware store. I went to the store and bought all they had—about twenty. I then drove the four miles to Antigua to another hardware store and bought all they had, which was about 175 buckets. We bought the three-and-a-half-gallon buckets since the five-gallon bucket, when filled with mud, was too heavy to haul. We got back to the volunteers, passed out the buckets, and set up the bucket brigades. This was the best we could do at the time, but it still resulted in speeding up the cleanup immensely. Many people had been just sitting around because they didn't have a shovel. Now, with the buckets, we put everyone to work and results came quickly. Fortunately, we didn't uncover any bodies, but not too far away some teams did.

We were able to get funds from Samaritan's Purse to buy blankets and steel roofing. The Vista Hermosa Rotary Club donated money for a lot of food and tools. John Sherrill and Jeff Reed donated funds to buy food staples, cleaning supplies, and buckets. For the next week, we worked with a women's organization to provide hot meals for the volunteer workers and the displaced families, mainly women and children. Thanks to donors, we bought about 1,000 buckets, food staples, blankets, and cleaning supplies, which we delivered to several Guatemalan departments. To the displaced people, each family was given a five-gallon bucket filled with food and another bucket with cleaning supplies. The buckets also included blankets, towels, hygiene items, and laundry soap. We went to four different departments with these and worked with the local women's organizations, which had already identified the affected families. In addition to the supplies, the families found uses for the buckets for years to come!

About this time, we received a call from Samaritan's Purse. They had workers in Guatemala City ready to fly out when the nearby volcano erupted. The Guatemala City airport was shut down for eight days. Instead of flying out, these workers came and helped us.

With Samaritan's Purse funds, we were able to buy 500 sheets of tin. Many families had lost part or all of their homes. We couldn't rebuild houses, but we were able to go to about ten different sites and give each family five sheets of tin so they could have at least some temporary shelter from the rain. In the

Department of Totonicapán, there was a father with six children that we were able to give food and blankets to. Not only had their house been washed away, but his wife (their mother) had also. The look on their faces will stay with me forever. "He that oppresseth the poor reproacheth his Maker: but he that honoureth him hath mercy on the poor." (Proverbs 14:31)

Again, we were shown God's providence. When disasters hit, it's time for Christians to respond. Many relief organizations limit themselves to a pre-planned budget and use that as a reason not to respond to disaster. Other issues exist, sometimes with boards of directors who are only focused on keeping costs down, not considering God in the equation. Step off by faith! We need to use God's provision, especially our budgets, when it's needed. We plan, always, to respond immediately and depend on God to provide.

Another of my brothers provided an amazing blessing in 2010. When my brother Steve and his wife Rhonda made the last payment on their house in Middleton, Wisconsin, they decided they were going to build a house for a widow and her three children. So they came to Guatemala and sponsored this house, and Ben was able to lead the team of volunteers. Steve and Rhonda also bought school uniforms for the two girls. What an honorable way to celebrate making their last house payment! Steve has been very active helping Chad and Cindy pick up wheelchairs in and around Middleton.

In the fall of 2011, I drove the Hope Haven twelve-and-half ton freightliner truck from Sioux Falls up to the Twin Cities area in Minnesota to pick up a donation of wheelchairs. About two hours from Sioux Falls, I stopped at the Elmendorf Hutterite colony in Mount Lake, Minnesota to pick up Herb Waldner. Herb was planning to introduce me to folks in another Hutterite colony near Minneapolis. That colony was called Altuna Colony and was located in Henderson, Minnesota. I completed my pick-ups in the Twin Cities, and came back to the Altuna Colony, which donated some steel roofing and trim from one of their businesses, Rush River Steel. Herb had joined Matt and I on a wheelchair delivery in Palestine a few years before.

It was just about dark on my way to drop Herb off at Elmendorf when I received a call to get home! Herb had some Spanish Bibles he wanted me to take, so I needed to stop and get them. By this time, I'd been on the road for over twelve hours and was ready to get home. I went into his carpentry shop; in the office, Joel Waldner introduced me to a Mennonite friend of his, Ed Landis.

"Mark, I want you to meet Ed. He's from Pennsylvania." Being in a hurry, I wanted to at least be polite, so I asked him where he was from.

Ed responded, "Lancaster County," and I told him that I used to live in Snyder County, Pennsylvania. Ed said his wife was from Snyder County.

I replied, "I used to live with the Eli Miller family."

"That's my wife's family."

I knew her! Eli had three daughters. One was already married when I lived with him. The twins, who were seventeen years old at the time, were Ruth and Rachel.

So I asked Ed, "What's her name, Ruth or Rachel?" He told me he was married to Ruth and asked if I'd like to meet her. He called and within five minutes she came into the shop.

I said, "Little sister, how are you?" in Pennsylvania Dutch. I asked about her parents and learned they had both passed away about ten years before.

Had Eli had a phone, I would have stayed in contact with him. I felt terrible that I had lost people so dear to me, even though I hadn't seen them since 1988 when they let us store that first trailer-load of wheelchairs at their farm when the truck broke down. From the time I was introduced to Ed, it only took about a minute to figure out that he was married to Ruth, the daughter of my adopted father back in the late 1970s. Yet another divine appointment!

In November 2012, we were hosting a wheelchair delivery team from the University of Mary in North Dakota. All of a sudden, the ground started to shake and we rushed everyone out of the building. The walls in the driveway outside the workshop appeared to be rolling. Within minutes, I called the Samaritan's Purse headquarters in North Carolina to let them know about the earthquake, just so it was on their radar. We received a call from William Sosa who worked for the Guatemalan Red Cross, and he gave us more information on the earthquake. There were concerns that it might cause a tsunami along the coast. We learned the epicenter was close to San Marcos.

Later that day, we were able to collect some wheelchairs, walkers, and blankets and filled up a pickup, which belonged to the Red Cross representative we'd worked with, to send immediately to San Marcos. We got a commitment from Samaritan's Purse to buy 1,000 blankets, so we put in an order and within a day or two, we had them from a local factory that took bolts of felt and cut them into blankets. Within a couple of days we filled our van, the pickup, and another van with blankets, hundreds of cases of Kids Against Hunger meals, and some foam mattresses, and we drove to San Marcos. We arrived at night and went to one of the sites where a large tent had been put up for the people who couldn't go back into their homes. Most of the men were walking around outside, and the women and children were huddled inside without enough blankets. At 7,000 feet elevation, it was very cold. One of the church volunteers whose house was unaffected let us sleep there, but even inside, we were still cold. The next day we quickly set up an organized distribution line based on families. Each family was given an adult and baby blanket and a couple of day's worth of food. World Vision had also shown up, along with some of the Red Cross volunteers.

The reality that really stuck out for Matt and me was the crumbled houses. All of the adobe houses were gone, and of the others left standing, most were at least cracked. Matt was amazed as he watched these wonderful people. Guatemalans are so resilient. In many ways, they are used to bad things happening. The beautiful thing is, if there was someone who needed help, the neighbors and others always helped out. In a matter of days, typical, life pretty much resumed.

The next day, Sosa took us to three different, smaller villages, which had been damaged and organized to bring in the affected families so that we could give them blankets, foods, and mattresses. Our first site was at a small office in a community and people were already in line waiting for us. Before we started giving away the blankets and food, we noticed a bunch of Red Cross boxes of hygiene supplies in another room. We were told they couldn't give them away until the Red Cross director from Guatemala came for a photo opportunity. By this time, people had been living outside for three nights. It made my blood boil that someone felt he was so important that all of these people had to suffer until he showed up. I was very, very impressed with the quality of the Red Cross volunteers. They demonstrated commitment and compassion. However, I was not impressed at all with the leadership.

We spent the remainder of the day distributing food to the other communities. We saw the damage in the homes. It was probably not the smartest thing, but we went into the homes. After the earthquake, there were aftershocks and homes were still vulnerable. On our way back to Antigua, about an hour into the trip, we saw that the Guatemalan army was arriving to help. It had troubled me that we couldn't get to the people earlier, but it made us feel good that we were able to get there before the army with supplies and comfort to help these poor families.

CHAPTER 19

BOUNTIFUL BLESSINGS

O ur ability to use the U.S. Navy's Project Handclasp was an amazing blessing in multiple ways. One of the biggest advantages was that they would fast track the wheelchairs through customs. But there were a few times when things didn't go as planned.

Once, we put about 300 wheelchairs on a ship that was supposed to take half of the chairs to Tanzania and the other half to Kenya. The wheelchairs were delivered to Dar Salaam, Tanzania, without any problem. But when the ship arrived in Mombasa, Kenya, they had a terrorist threat and were forced to pull up anchor and head to the U.S. military base in Rota, Spain. After a year of hoping and praying the wheelchairs would make it on another ship to Kenya, we agreed to have Project Handclasp return them to the States. Before long, they were on a ship to Norfolk, Virginia.

I asked the Navy, "If we procured a container for Kenya, would you take the wheelchairs off of the pallets and load a forty-foot sea container for Kenya?"

If we had to have them palletized and put on the truck to be shipped back to Iowa, and then shipped back to a port, the combined extra expense would be between $5,000 and $6,000. So I called Steve and Julie Farris who traveled with us back in the early 1970s. They were now living in Newport News, Virginia. I explained our predicament, and they said, "Well, our daughter and son-in-law own one of the largest nurseries on the East Coast and have semis and loading docks just west of the Navy yard."

So we scheduled a sea container to arrive in late March, as I needed to be at the annual board meeting for Children's Medical Ministries in the D.C. area. I flew into Norfolk and was picked up by Steve Farris, and just like clock work, we were able to cross stuff the chairs from their semi into the sea container. The wheelchairs were badly needed in Kenya.

Another time, we shipped two semi-trucks with over 400 wheelchairs to Biloxi, Mississippi to go to Armenia, Colombia. I was in Guatemala at the Hope Haven Guatemala factory in Santo Domingo Xenacoj one afternoon—not too long after this—and I received a call from the head of Project Handclasp telling me that they just learned that the U.S.S. Sacagawea was too big to make it into the Port of Cartagena.

"Could they just drop the wheelchairs in Chile?"

I told them this was unacceptable and made a few calls to our partners in Colombia who were Rotarians that we were well connected with. So they got together with the Colombian Navy and convinced them to take a smaller ship out to where the Sacagawea was anchored. They transferred the wheelchairs to the port and onto trucks, which took them to Armenia in time for the Hope Haven West team to do the seating clinic. I have learned not to get frustrated because if we wait on the Lord, things work out better than how we planned them. "The Lord is good unto them that wait for him, to the soul that seeketh him." (Lamentations 3:25)

While in the Air Force, Richard St. Denis broke his back in a snow skiing accident and has used a wheelchair ever since. Richard became active in wheelchair sports and met some of our team members when coming here to Guatemala in November 1999 for the Association of Mobility Provider's conference. Being open to new ideas, Richard saw the value of this conference and joined us for five days. He later started facilitating sports camps in Mazatlan, Mexico. He eventually moved to Mexico, just north of Mexico City, and founded the World Access Project. Richard became one of the CNN heroes of 2011.

Richard had lots of interest from people who saw the CNN story. He had created awareness just for the fact that he had set up a wheelchair repair shop in Mexico. He had a team from the board on his church in Mariposa, California go down to Mexico. I flew down to join them for three or four days and was very impressed with their attention to detail when putting children and adults in wheelchairs.

In addition, one of the community outreaches they were doing was to build a wheelchair ramp, therefore enabling the recipient to get into his home, something that is almost always overlooked when delivering wheelchairs. For them, it was all about fostering independence. Richard and I set a day aside to go up to San Juan, Del Rio, to visit a wheelchair factory called Bertha. The shop partnered with Whirlwind Wheelchairs and built a version of the Rough Rider wheelchair, one of Ralf Hodgkiss's innovations. One thing that amazed me was that they would make their own wheels and lace their own spokes from the wheel hub to the rim. The workers in that part of the shop were all deaf. It was impressive to see the camaraderie in their work. On our way home, we stopped in Temascalcingo to see the mayor.

Richard had been working with the wife of the mayor in Temascalcingo, a town of about 20,000 people and off the beaten path but very close to the highway that intersects Puebla with Guadalajara. He was trying to set up a meeting with the mayor because he wanted to get three to five acres of land donated by the town so he could create a sports' complex and a wheelchair shop.

By this time he had done many wheelchair sports camps all over central Mexico. So in addition to moving the shop to that location, he would also be able to hold the sports' camps there. The mayor's wife was in charge of the local DIF, which basically meant Integral Family Development. While we were in the meeting with the mayor and his staff, Richard was making his plea but not making much progress. I pulled out a folder and showed the mayor a picture of the new Hope Haven Guatemala facility we were just about to move into. When he saw the picture of an 18,000-square-foot warehouse, he said, "I have an idea. Follow me."

We drove about a mile to a multi-use building, which was basically a Quonset-hut type gymnasium. It was 18,000-square-feet and empty at that time with the exception of some food storage bins for poor farmers. The mayor asked, "What if I donated this building to you?" We couldn't believe it! This was an absolute dream come true.

Within four or five months, Richard had moved into this location and has kept it through future city administrations, his free lease always being renewed. About once or twice a year we'd send a couple hundred refurbished wheelchairs from Iowa. We also did a pilot project where we shipped 400 Hope Haven KidChairs so he and his staff could do final assembly. From there, those chairs were distributed through Richard and other partners throughout Mexico. In the environment we were in, I can't tell you what an amazing blessing the gift of this building was! This was a perfect scenario. Even if he could have afforded to buy the land, the legal complications of foreigners owning land were prohibitive. If the land had been donated, he would have needed a capital campaign to build, which most likely would have taken three to four years. This donation was a true blessing from the Lord!

Karen Rispin was a missionary kid who was raised in Kenya in the1960s where she went to a Christian boarding school in the Rift Valley in Kijabe. Karen went on to become a professor of biology at LeTourneau University in Longview, Texas. In Kenya, the British had developed the whole boarding school concept for children and adapted that concept for children with disabilities. Joytown was a boarding school primarily for children with spina bifida. Karen had a heart for Kenya and around 2012, she decided there needed to be a comparison study done so that wheelchair providers could improve the wheelchairs they offered. She decided to conduct the study using the different wheelchairs currently being provided.

She started with the Joni and Friends Regency chair, which was a knockoff of the Hope Haven KidChair. Because JAF's main supervisor's core competency was welding, they used a similar concept of what we had done except they welded the frame together. It was not quite as durable, but they made it in only the smaller size, so it didn't have to have to carry the same weight load as a bigger chair. They took twenty-five Regency chairs and compared them with twenty-five African-made chairs, made in Nairobi by an organization called African Persons with Disabilities in Kenya (ADPK). They put students in the chairs and came back six months later to do a follow-up evaluation on durability, rolling resistance, how easy it was to push, and the ease of getting in and out of it. Karen then asked me to provide twenty-five Hope Haven KidChairs in the fourteen-inch configuration to be compared to the ADPK chair. For the most part, the Hope Haven KidChair outperformed the others. Their biggest concern was how it made contact with the ground. When on rugged terrain, only three of the four wheels were making contact with the ground since it was on a rigid frame. So the recommendation we were given, because of this study, was to consider building a three-wheeled frame chair.

I designed the BeeLine chairs with that children's chair in mind. Karen's husband Phil was also a professor at LeTourneau in the missionary aviation department. Karen went back every spring with some wheelchairs for the kids in Joytown. There were over 300 children at Joytown, which of course was the perfect location for doing this research. In 2017, Karen and Phil established a non-profit called AT (Assistive Technology) Catalyst. They resigned their positions at the university at the end of the school year to be full-time missionaries. Their goal was for the mission hospitals to get more wheelchairs in Kijabe and Tenwek, hospitals established one hundred years ago. Her goal was that by working through the hospitals, she'd be able to use wheelchairs as one way to show the love of Jesus.

In 2015, I was getting very concerned with our partners at PET International (now Mobility Worldwide) regarding the speed (or lack thereof) with which they were responding to concerns coming back from the field. Mel West, Larry Hills, and Earl Miner had designed the original PET wheelchair for the lowlands of the sub-Saharan in the rainforest of Africa. In that area of the world, there are mainly dirt roads. The chair was very heavy and slow, yet durable. On our more recent distributions, more and more people refused to take the PET in favor of a standard wheelchair. Even though the PET made it easier for users to have a business selling and hauling things, it was too long and clunky to use inside their homes.

I had been working with Kirby Goering from PET Kansas to lead the design of a PET with three speeds, using an internal hub. The leadership at PET was willing to consider this design, but only in the old, heavy model. A few prototypes were made—and even field-tested—but the chairs were never built for distribution. Next, they brought on Rod Miner, an expert in bike technology and owner of Lightfoot Cycles. His father, Earl, had helped with the early PET design. They told Rod he could only design a three-speed if he used the heavy steel wood base. He was set up to fail from the beginning.

Soon, Maurice Haff contacted me. She is an engineering professor at Central Oklahoma University who asked me to look at a wheelchair that was more of a seat one sits on with his or her knees. Matt and I stopped to see him when driving one of the donated wheelchair lift vans to Guatemala from the Marianjoy Hospital in Wheaton, Illinois. The seat was at an angle, and the rider rested on his knees. They used a 1¼" perforated tube, but rather than telescoping it, they used flat steel with a hole every inch and used lots of tube. I could immediately envision how this could work and told the professor and students my thoughts.

The next time I was back in Rock Valley, Iowa, I remembered years before, Cal De Ryder from Siouxland Fabricating had shown me a laser cutter they had acquired. I knew little about these high-tech computer-controlled machines, so I went to Cal's office and told him I needed some sample plates cut with square holes for carriage bolts.

He said, "Come with me," and took me to the office of their engineer, Jeff Kock, stating that he was the best and would help. We soon had some pieces ready to test.

At first, we had to cut round washers with square holes to accommodate the ¼" shoulder on the standard 7/16" carriage bolt. It wasn't long until we learned it would be easier to have them lathed to length at the Mike Durfee State Penitentiary in Springfield, South Dakota. I worked with the PET shop in nearby Hawarden, Iowa to modify the angle on the hand crank to fit onto the Bumblebee, our new chair. I thought, "Why not put a castor on the front, so if the hand crank assembly was taken off you would have an active three-wheeled wheelchair?" I came up with the idea of a square tube telescoping. I bought some tubing and made a bit of progress.

Taking the three-wheeled active chair design, I was able to consult with our wheelchair users in Guatemala, as well as some in the United States, and let them try it out. We realized we were onto something that might meet the needs of people who needed an all-terrain, active wheelchair. Having an active chair meant that you could change the wheel camber, the wheel size, the seat dump (angle), the center of gravity, and the length of the wheelbase, which would be an amazing accomplishment. It wasn't long until we had designed a "seat to back" bracket that provided a sturdy support as well as angling adjustability. By now, we had an active chair that could be attached to a single speed hand crank, a tow bar to attach the chair behind a bicycle, and a trailer for hauling cargo.

A public relations firm in Sioux Falls, Lawrence and Schiller, has done a lot of work for Hope Haven, and they offered to do the logo and trademark for us. They incorporated the concepts and names of the Bumblebee, Honeybee, and the idea of the worker bee and came up with the "Beeline" to incorporate all of these chairs. They used an attorney to trademark the name Beeline. Not long after this, I was in meetings in California showing the Bumblebee and the Honeybee to David and his staff at Global Mobility, including Executive Director Chris Grange. Chris had been a pastor at a Presbyterian church in South Bay, California and one of Chris's ex-parishioners was an attorney that taught the patent class at the UCLA School of Law. We had a meeting at UCLA, and they offered to do the patent work pro bono. We applied for a utility patent, a patent that covers the creation of a new or improved, useful product, process or machine.

We also received help from students at LeTourneau University. Their senior design team, Frontier Wheelchairs, was made up of the students from their engineering program. These students helped us with some initial testing of the new design. The first test showed us the need to improve the back.

Testing is essential when developing wheelchairs. In 2011, I had been involved with a lot of wheelchair organizations, the World Health Organization (WHO), and USAID in putting together some wheelchair guidelines. The first thing they did was come up with a definition of a wheelchair. A wheelchair is more than just an aid to mobility. It can be a means to self-sufficiency and increased self-esteem; it may be a vehicle to meaningful employment and contributions to community and society; and it reduces dependency and the associated burden placed on family and friends. A wheelchair is so critical to someone with limited mobility. We needed to acknowledge the benefits and necessity of wheelchairs in the lives of so many.

The one feature we were never able to design into our Hope Haven KidChair was the tilt-in-space mechanism. Our goal was to allow the user to tilt-in-space, and in addition, to have a recline feature, which would be an added blessing. Many children need to be put into tilt so they can breathe better, have better weight distribution, experience pressure relief, and rest more comfortably. We spent over twelve years trying to make the KidChair tilt and recline easily. We did accomplish putting it into permanent tilt, which was fine for some children. We managed to come up with a seat post clamp—kind of like a bicycle where you can adjust a seat and release wheels. It was a similar concept, although much stronger. We learned the Honeybee chair could be turned into a tilt-in-space chair and by adding the right holes to the back brackets, we could adjust the angle and even tilt it back into a gurney with the footrest coming up to support the feet. This was especially essential for children with osteogenesis imperfecta, or "brittle bone disease."

One of the challenges with wheelchairs that tilt-in-space is that when you tilt them back, you move the center of gravity, so you risk the wheelchair becoming prone to falling over backwards. This new, unique design allowed us to move the seat forward by increments, eliminating the need for an anti-tip wheel in the back of the chair. We were on our way!

Also in 2015, Pastor James Butler passed away in August in Missoula, Montana. James was a pastor for fifty-eight years, and his passion had been sharing the gospel of Jesus Christ. He had pastored for many years in Horseshoe Beach, Florida.

A little over a month before his death, during the July 4th weekend, I was delivering Ben's camper van to him. Ben took me to the Bitterroot National Forest on a father-son camping trip to show me some of the mountains he had been climbing. This was the same place that Jim Roberts had learned of the

House of Jesus from Rufus Sherrill. We went through Hamilton, Montana and camped on the perimeter. Ben is a traditional rock climber, and has spent a lot of time in this area, including Blodgett Canyon. We got up early and went to the Missoula Farmers Market and visited with Tamara Kittelson, an occupational therapist that we had worked with for many years, and her husband Rick.

Next we went up to Trout Creek, Montana. We found James and spent some time talking with him, reliving fond memories of the early years in ministry. He had been a close friend of Jim Roberts, my former pastor and the leader of The Assembly. We were in agreement with how Jim had taken what had been a good "call of God" movement and turned it into his own personal cult, one that hurt a lot of people. I'm still grateful for that last visit with this incredible man of God.

Ben and I went hiking in Glacier National Park, and then I went back to Sioux Falls. A little over a month later, we recieved word that James was on his way to the hospital, having had a severe heart attack. There was a huge network of people praying for him, but before another day had gone by, he'd gone to be with the Lord. I was able to go to his funeral in Cross City, Florida, along with people from all over the country. It was the most powerful funeral I'd ever attended, where people whose lives had been changed through James's obedience to the Lord gave testimony. There was a supper, followed by worship with singing that evening.

While eating, I was able to talk to a dear friend I hadn't seen since he was living with the Amish, thirty-five years before. Michael had become a successful businessman in Tennessee. I was telling him about some children who needed wheelchairs in Cuba and Kenya and a little bit about the new Beeline that was being developed. He asked me what it would cost if he wanted to sponsor some wheelchairs and how sponsorship worked. I told him it was about $250 per wheelchair. I assumed he might want to sponsor five or ten chairs, so gave quotes thinking in those terms. I felt like Abraham negotiating with the Lord. Instead of lowering the numbers, he kept upping them. "Well, what if I wanted to sponsor ten chairs? How about twenty?" He ended up sponsoring one hundred chairs. We needed to get a bunch of wheelchairs to Kenya for the children at Joytown. Michael's gift, made possible by God's divine intervention of connecting with him at James's funeral, made it possible to help one hundred children in Kenya.

James Butler had moved a few years before he died from Horseshoe Beach, Florida to Trout Creek, Montana with his daughter and son-in-law, Jeff. Jeff Reed had sold his portion of a steel company in Florida and purchased a cattle ranch in western Montana. More than ten years before, I had worked with James's sons-in-law, John and Jeff, who were co-owners of the steel company, Gulf Coast Steel and Manufacturing. I had contacted them about helping us with some steel roofing. The wheelchair repair shop that Chito and I founded in Chimaltenango had developed some terrible leaks in the roof, causing an open section that needed to be covered. I requested they come from Florida and help us redo the roof. The Gulf Coast team went to Guatemala to assess the roof and left money with the folks there to buy the steel trussing that was needed. I worked with them to get all of the pieces of steel roofing shipped down on a container with wheelchairs. When everything was in place, they came down, and in just a week, totally recovered the roof.

While there John's son, Jonathan Sherrill, who led the team saw that many poor people were living in houses with rusty tin roofs and cornstalk walls. He discussed these living conditions with me, noting that the carports that they built in Florida were much better than the houses that these poor people lived in. So he sent down a few modified carport sides with insulation, shipping them with some wheelchairs. We put them up for a couple of the families. After finishing these houses, I realized that there needed to be better air circulation, a few windows, rain gutters, and they needed to be a little bigger.

These carports turned out to be the prototype that evolved into the "Relief Home." We went through about six different modifications until we were satisfied with a model. By the end of 2009, we had dialed into what we felt was a model we could stick use.

This was yet another example in my life of God's incredible plan. Because of a leaky roof, the entire Relief Home project was developed. Divine intervention was starting to feel like the normal course of my life! God uses situations that might look difficult or irritating in order to provide blessings. Our faith in Him, in spite of seemingly pointless difficulties, provides the base on which He can build His kingdom. Trust in the Lord, always! "Who comforteth us in all our tribulation, that we may be able to comfort them which are in any trouble, by the comfort wherewith we ourselves are comforted of God." (2 Cor. 1:4)

Now we're doing so well in Guatemala that we are able to serve other developing nations. We've been looking into serving in Peru and have been working with the government in the Moquegua province near Chile, Bolivia, and Ecuador.

CHAPTER 20

FUTURE GROWTH

I n the New Testament, Jesus gives us both The Great Commission, to go into the entire world and make disciples, but he also gave us the Great Commandment, to love our neighbors as ourselves. In my experience, the 21st-century church has tried to separate these two and put a division between evangelistic mission agencies and relief and development agencies. I don't believe you can present the Great Commission without incorporating the Great Commandment because the two go hand in hand. I am very fortunate to be surrounded by people from all walks of life who have taken Jesus seriously when he says to love your neighbor as yourself. In Matthew 22:36-40, it's laid out quite clearly. "Master, which is the great commandment in the law?' Jesus said unto him, 'Thou shalt love the Lord thy God with all thy heart, and with all thy soul, and with all thy mind. This is the first and great commandment. And the second is like unto it, Thou shalt love thy neighbour as thyself.'"

When I lived with the Amish, they looked down on organizations that were only relief agencies because they saw them as just presenting a social rather than spiritual gospel. I think it was a tactic of the devil to sow discord and divide God's people into two camps when really there is only one. Unfortunately, many organizations pray for people and preach to them but are not effective because they do not "love their neighbors" as they should. All we have to do is to look at Jesus as an example. Yes, he preached, but he also met their needs.

Being led by the Lord is not just a 1st-century concept. From my time as a homeless teenager, to my years hitchhiking and hopping freights around the country as part of the radical Jesus movement, to living with the Plain people who were much like people lived in the 18th and 19th centuries, and to living with the primitive Mayans in the jungles and highlands of Central America, I've learned that being in a place where you have to trust the Lord and depend on Him for all of your needs is a spiritually healthy thing. It brings us to our knees to pray when we feel helpless. I've learned that when we put ourselves in a position to be used by the Lord, we can see His miracles all around us. In America, we have so many safety nets these days, so people often don't find themselves in a position where they have to truly rely on God.

In the last chapter of the book of Mark, we discover what should be the norm for one who believes. In order to be useful to God, we need to put on the full armor of God. Unless we are in a place of great need, most of us don't realize the importance of these amazing tools the Lord gives us. After nearly five decades of striving to walk with Jesus, I now—more than ever—see the need to put on the whole armor of God every day, in every situation. In Mark 16:16–18, Jesus speaks about true religion. "He that believeth and is baptized shall be saved; but he that believeth not shall be damned. And these signs shall follow them that believe; In my name shall they cast out devils; they shall speak with new tongues; They shall take up serpents; and if they drink any deadly thing, it shall not hurt them; they shall lay hands on the sick, and they shall recover."

I feel like I'm so far from the Christian norm in our country. For instance, we shouldn't think it's strange to see miracles all of the time. God is the same yesterday, today, and tomorrow. In a well-balanced Christian life, love and service, hand and hand, in God's kingdom should be our priority. In Matthew 6:33, Jesus says it clearly, "But seek ye first the kingdom of God, and his righteousness; and all these things shall be added unto you."

Micah 6:8 remonstrates, "He hath shewed thee, O man, what is good; and what doth the Lord require of thee, but to do justly, and to love mercy, and to walk humbly with thy God?" To obey is better than sacrifice (1 Samuel 15:22) and true religion is to visit the fatherless and widows in their affliction (James 1:27). These verses have challenged me. I've fallen short of them, but I've tried to apply them to my life.

I believe many times, we over-plan each step of our life, and that's okay as long as we step aside to let God modify our plans. Many ministries can't see past their budgets and their mission statements. Sometimes, I've found that God tears up our mission statement and modifies it. An example would be the time we had the back-to-back tropical storm and earthquake. Our projected wheelchair production goals had to be modified. It was more important to use our time and resources to help those in immediate need. I would like to challenge all ministries to avoid making excuses for not having the resources or gifts to obey His calling. He just wants obedience. He can provide because He has "the cattle on a thousand hills."

And now, my life is taking another turn as I respond to a call from the Lord. The Hope Haven KidChair has blessed many children with a simple, durable wheelchair that serves moderately disabled children and young adults, meeting the need for a tilt-in-space feature that serves both small and larger children, as well as adults with complex seating needs. The need for a wheelchair that could be configured in so many ways has been met with the KidChair.

This is how the Beeline was birthed. In 2018, Hope Haven agreed to release me and bless me so I could pursue my passion and calling to develop the Beeline. It had been a challenge for all of us at Hope Haven to continue the research and development. In light of all of the domestic funding cuts Hope Haven was facing at home, I felt the call. So, I resigned from my responsibilities at Hope Haven International and Hope Haven Guatemala. I still partner with them, but I am no longer an employee.

I have been so blessed by my years working with Hope Haven and will miss them all. There are many Christian rehabilitation centers in the United States, but it was Hope Haven that stuck their neck out all those years ago to add an international ministry. God has honored their faith and because of that obedience, hundreds of thousands of people worldwide have been blessed.

And last, I'd like to mention the importance of being a servant. As a young Christian in the early Jesus movement, I found there were a lot of people more interested in understanding future fulfillment of prophecy rather than just giving their life to Jesus in service and follow his lead. I learned early on that as a young Christian, you're just going to frustrate yourself trying to predict the future. Instead, in Revelations 1:1, Jesus talks about prophecy. "The Revelation of Jesus Christ, which God gave unto him, to shew unto his servants things which must shortly come to pass; and he sent and signified it by his angel unto his servant John." The prophecy that is shared with us is in the Bible. Unless you're serving him, don't try to understand the deeper mysteries and the future. I realized that I just needed to obey God and serve him by being obedient to help the poor. One thing I failed at, my biggest regret, was sometimes getting too busy to pray. I thank Him for surrounding me with others that have faithfully prayed and are praying for me. Here is another group of my heroes. Yes, we have to actively serve God, but I know I also need to pray and maintain a close walk with Him. He can and will use anybody, but it's important that we're like David and be men (and women) after God's own heart. Not like someone who doesn't fail God, but a person who is willing to repent and make things right. Humility and submission will always result in the Lord's leading.

And now, trusting in the Lord each step of the way, I start my new journey.

PHOTO COLLECTION II

Surrounding our mother, Betty, and Grandmother Mary. I wish
Grandmother would have shared more about her Dustbowl
refugee days, but it was too painful for her to talk about.

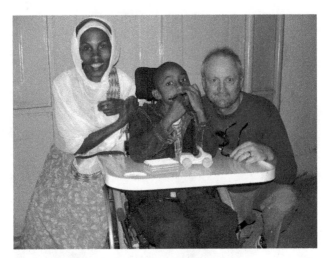

Philip Haney gives a harmonica to a young boy in Asmara, Eretria.

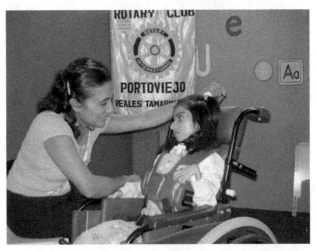

All over the world, we see the love a mother has
for her children, regardless of their condition.

Top row: David, Mark. Next row: Ilse Caballeros, Risna Utami (now Risna Richard). In June of 2016 we participated in a panel that was narrated by Candice Cable at the UN's Convention on the rights of persons with disabilities. Candice was a Paralympic athlete that has won eight gold medals and won the Boston Marathon six times in the women's wheelchair division.

In Cusco, Peru on a Rotary-sponsored wheelchair delivery with the Cusco Rotary Club and Modesto, California area clubs.

Matt giving blankets to victims of the San Marcos,
Guatemala earthquake where we helped Samaritan's Purse
and Kids Against Hunger feed 500 families in two days.

We built a Relief Home for this family. The young mother had arthritis and could
barely prepare meals for her family. We had a team from Hope Haven Canada
build this from a couple of incomplete kits and they did an amazing job.

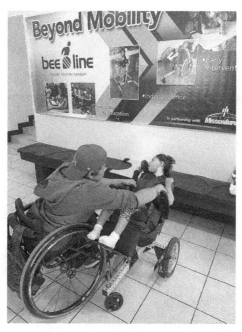

The amazing thing about the Honeybee wheelchair is how comfortable a child can be if the technician takes the time to get everything adjusted to the right size and angle. Gustavo lives in constant pain, so he knows the importance of a properly adjusted wheelchair.

I worshipped with the Amish friends I'd lived with many years before, as well as their children and grandchildren.

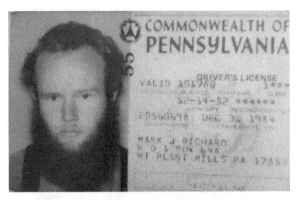

Even though I lived with Old Order Plain people in the late 1970's and early 1980's, because I had never joined any of their churches I was not forbidden from having a driver's license.

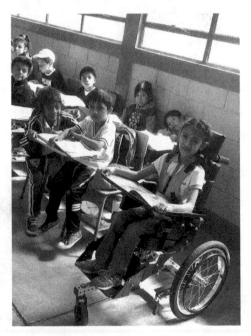

Darly at school in Xenacoj. She would soon have a computer so that she could communicate better with her classmates.

Hungry children started eating what our team left on their plates while we were
at the beach after finishing up a wheelchair delivery on the coast of Guatemala.
Nearly 78% of the children in Guatemala live below the poverty line.

Tommy Lasorda with Matt, Michael, and
Ben in 1997 in his office at Dodger Stadium.

*Matt overseeing the construction of a Relief Home for
a widow and her children in Santo Domingo, Xenacoj.*

*Our team from Canada and the US are given
a tour of a rehab hospital in North Vietnam.*

Dr. Lana Svien developed a faculty lead program to bring large groups of OT and PT students from the University of South Dakota to Guatemala and other countries.

Michael, two years old, at the Mayan Ruins of Copan in Honduras.

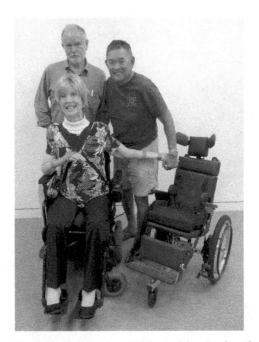

*Mark, Joni Eareckson Tada and her husband
Ken admiring the Honeybee wheelchair.*

Ten years later, Mark and the woman who inspired the first wheelchair, Marcaria.

ABOUT THE AUTHORS

Mark Richard is currently manufacturing the Beeline wheelchairs in partnership with Mission Impact in Santo Domingo Xenacoj, Guatemala. Mark started bringing used wheelchairs to Guatemala in 1988. Over the years, he has founded and co-founded many ministries that deliver wheelchairs. They spent over ten years sorting different makes and models of donated wheelchairs, training volunteer shops to specialize in refurbishing the different types, and then strategically shipping certain types of wheelchairs to over 100 different countries in order to make the deliveries easier. Seeing the need to standardize and simplify this process, Mark started to manufacture appropriate wheelchairs. In 2018, Mark abandoned refurbishing old wheelchairs after developing the Beeline wheelchair, which can meet the needs of wheelchair users with complex seating needs for infants to adults.

In his youth, Mark was part of the hippy, anti-war generation, and by 1971 he immersed himself into the radical Jesus movement. Eventually he became part of a revival among the Old Order Amish, Mennonites, and German Baptists, which brought him to Central America. There he learned community development and mission work with the Mayans in the jungles of Belize and the highlands of

Guatemala. His stories of God's salvation during those years are truly amazing. Enabled by an amazing cast of friends and colleagues, God has used his strengths and weaknesses to develop a ministry that has been life-changing for so many. Mark currently resides in Guatemala with his wife and canine buddies, tirelessly developing and distributing wheelchairs to people whose lives change when they receive them. In addition, they spend a few weekends a month at their coffee farm in the rain forest in northern Guatemala.

Beeline can be found at www.beelinewheelchairs.org and Mark's Beeline Wheelchairs Facebook page.

———————

June Gaston is a former teacher and administrator in public school settings in Nebraska and South Dakota. During this time, she completed her doctorate in educational administration and helped to start the first Spanish immersion school in South Dakota. June first got to know Mark in the mountains of Ecuador while on a mission trip, delivering wheelchairs to people without any mobility options. While bumping along the mountain roads, she heard Mark's amazing life story and encouraged him to write it out someday to encourage others that, in Mark's words, "If God can use me, He can use anybody!"

As the years passed, June and Mark stayed in touch, and after her retirement, Mark contacted her. Others had encouraged him to share his story of God's amazing interventions in a life that could just as easily been one lived in prison. They started working on his story in Sioux Falls and via technology when Mark was somewhere else in the world—which was often! Although this is the first book June has written, she spent much of her career in educational writing endeavors and has always loved to write. Pairing this opportunity with her love for God has been a dream come true. Blessed with a loving husband, children and grandchildren, June loves to spend her time writing, reading, and making feeble attempts to play the violin.

ENDNOTES

Behring, Kenneth E. *The Road to Leadership: Finding a Life of Purpose.* Adelaide, South Australia: Blackhawk Press, 2013.

Bunyan, John. *Pilgrim's Progress.* Grand Rapids: Zondervan, 1966.

Braght, Thieleman J. van, and Joseph F. Sohm. (1987). *The bloody theater, or, Martyrs' mirror.* Scottdale, Pa: Herald Press.

Card, Michael. "The Gentle Healer." *Scandalon,* Sparrow Records, 1986. Online https://genius.com/Michael-card-the-gentle-healer-lyrics, accessed Sept. 29, 2019.

Eareckson Tada, Joni. Program #3575, Aired 1/12/96, *A need for pediatric wheelchairs: children and disabilities #5.*

Ember Days. "Real Jesus." *More Than You Think,* Come & Live, 2013. Online https://genius.com/The-ember-days-real-jesus-lyrics, accessed Oct. 1, 2019.

Foxe, John. *Foxe's Book of Martyrs.* England: John Day, 1563.

Griffin, John Howard. *Black Like Me.* Boston: Houghton Mifflin Harcourt, 1961.

Guerra, Jim. (2000). *From Dean's List to Dumpsters: Why I Left Harvard to Join a Cult.* Pittsburgh, Pennsylvania: Dorance Publishing Company.

Hoffman, Abbie. *Steal This Book.* New York City: Grove Press, 1971.

Krotz, Joanna I. "Philanthropy A New Breed." *Town & Country*, June 2005, pp190–191.

McGuire, Barry. "Eve of Destruction." *Eve of Destruction,* Dunhill Records, 1965. https://genius.com/Barry-mcguire-eve-of-destruction-lyrics, accessed Sept. 29, 2019.

Mullins, Rich. "You Did Not Have a Home." *The Jesus Record,* Word Entertainment, 2010. Online https://genius.com/Rich-mullins-you-did-not-have-a-home-demo-version-lyrics, accessed Oct. 1, 2019.

Popov, Haralan. *Tortured For His Faith.* Grand Rapids: Zondervan, 1972.

Reader's Digest. *Wheels of Hope.* May 1997, pp. 31–32.

Sawyer, Diane. (1998-03-25). The Brethren." *Primetime* (ABC).

Sainte-Marie, Buffy. "Universal Soldier." *The Universal Soldier,* Amadeo, 1965. https://genius.com/Donovan-universal-soldier-lyrics, accessed Sept. 29, 2019.

Rubin, Jerry. *DO IT: Scenarios of the Revolution.* New York City: Simon and Schuster, 1970.

Stoll, John D. *Inside the Amish Riddle.* Scottdale, PA: Finger on the Wall, 2013.

Wikipedia contributors, "Country Joe McDonald," *Wikipedia, The Free Encyclopedia,* https://en.wikipedia.org/w/index.php?title=Country_Joe_McDonald&oldid=916126800, accessed October 1, 2019.

CPSIA information can be obtained
at www.ICGtesting.com
Printed in the USA
JSHW040200310321
13049JS00001B/32

9 781631 952241